Havanese
Dog

Ultimate New Owner's Guide.
Loving, Training, Feeding,
Grooming, Finding, Raising,
Socializing & Making Your Puppy
Into a Healthy and Happy Dog

Josip Bolg

Table of Contents

3

Introduction

Do you want to own a dog with a genuinely friendly and playful personality? Then you can never go wrong if you go for the Havanese dog breed, the national dog of Cuba. The cool personality of this breed is the reason why they are famous for being incredible pets and companions.

However, you should remember that just like other dog breeds, you also have to commit to taking good care of your Havanese if you have decided to make one as a pet. You have to know exactly how to tend to his needs. Moreover, you need to be able to commit some time and effort to ensure that he is well-groomed and stays on top of his health.

Fortunately, you now have this book to give you a comprehensive guide when it comes to caring for a Havanese. The good thing about this book is that it has a wide coverage. It covers almost everything you need to know about the breed so both you and your pet will have a smooth-sailing experience together.

It even teaches you ways to groom your Havanese, which is one of the trickiest parts involved in caring for this breed. The reason is that the Havanese is known for having a long, double coat, which may interfere with his vision and lead to painful mats if you do not take care of it. You can avoid such a problem with the information and advice included in this book.

Aside from that, it is up-to-date. It has all the updated information about feeding, training, and protecting him. At the end of this book, you will come out as a real expert when it comes to rearing your Havanese and making both your experiences together as unforgettable and enjoyable as possible.

Let's begin!

Chapter 1 – Fun and Exciting Facts About the National Dog of Cuba, The Havanese

A national dog of Cuba, the Havanese is a dog breed well-loved not only in the country where it came from but also in other parts of the world. There are definitely several good reasons why this breed continues to receive love from millions of people globally. Apart from being an amazing toy dog and lap dog, the Havanese is also a great companion. As a matter of fact, many view the Havanese as the perfect breed for anyone who wants to snuggle up with a pet after a long and tiring day.

This breed is also famous for being a performer, thanks to his playful and active personality. In other words, you can't expect him to be content if you rear him only as a lap dog. With his active personality, he will most likely move around and try to learn new and cool tricks. This can make training him a lot more enjoyable.

Origin/History

Also called Bichon Havanais and Havana Silk Dog, the Havanese dog breed has a somewhat exciting history. In 1942, Spanish settlers went to Cuba together with their small lap dogs. Isolated from other dogs because they live on the island and due to some trade restrictions, these lapdogs were interbred until the time when they evolved and got a more homogenous look. This mirrors the look of the Havanese breed recognized by the whole world today.

The breed was well-loved, especially by wealthy Cuban families as well as those who visit the island from England, Spain, and France. The fondness of foreign visitors to this breed, which is mainly brought on by the dog's adorable look, is one reason why the Havanese also became popular in Europe. They specifically love the long and silky fur or hair of the dog, which keeps them insulated from the heat of the tropical sun while remaining light and soft to touch.

However, the popularity of the Havanese also dropped all of a sudden during the 1950s. It is mainly due to the Cuban Revolution that took place during that time. The breed almost disappeared and only around 11 of them were taken to the US in 1959.

During the 70s, several American breeders were enchanted by the offspring of the eleven dogs brought there. This prompted them to restore the popularity of the Havanese. This saved the breed from possible extinction. Now, it continues to capture the hearts of a lot of dog lovers from different parts of the world.

Interesting Facts About the Havanese

Apart from its incredible history, there are also some facts about the Havanese that make it even more interesting. Here are just a few of them:

- **The Havanese is the only native dog breed in Cuba** – The breed came from Havana, a city in Cuba where its name was derived. As mentioned earlier, it nearly got extinct during the Cuban Revolution but got its popularity back eventually after US breeders became familiar with the few ones brought to the country.

- **The Havanese was developed from an extinct dog** – This breed actually came from the dog called Blanquito de la Habana, which is already extinct at present. With that, it truly has its roots in Cuba. It was cross-bred with different bichon dogs, like the poodle, to make the friendly and cute toy dog recognized in the world today, the Havanese.

- **The Havanese has a silky coat, which serves a purpose** – One noticeable feature of this breed is the long and silky coat. It looks quite warm but note that adding warmth is not its sole purpose. It is also meant to provide the breed with protection. What this coat does is offer a protective barrier against the heat of the sun, thereby preventing the dog from overheating.

- **The dog breed is easy to train** – Another interesting fact about the Havanese is that despite its small size, it is easy to train. As a matter of fact, some of them undergo training as service dogs. A Havanese was even approved to be part of the Hearing Ear Program in Great Britain just recently. The goal is to train him as a service dog meant to help the hearing impaired. The fact that they are easy to train is also one reason why you can see some of them being used to sniff out pests, like termites and mold.

- **Some famous personalities own Havanese dogs** – Among the famous personalities who became Havanese parents are Barbara Walters, Queen Anne, Ernest Hemingway, Charles Dickens, Queen Victoria, Joan Rivers, and Venus Williams. This means that this breed enchants also those who belong to the rich and the famous.

- **The Havanese is a great companion for those with allergies** – The silky hair of this breed tends to grow continuously, making it less irritating than the usual dog fur. With that, the Havanese is surely a fantastic dog for those who are often allergic to dogs. However, you should still remember that similar to other dogs, the Havanese tends to shed, so you cannot consider it as completely hypoallergenic.

- **The Havanese gets easily attached to owners** – Another nice thing about this breed is that they love to stick to their owners. They tend to get easily attached to their owners, which is why they earned the reputation of being the "Velcro dog". With that, expect these dogs to act as true companions capable of offering cuddles to their human masters.

- **The Havanese can live long** – The long lifespan of most Havanese dogs is also one of their most striking qualities. Despite being categorized as a toy breed, the Havanese is still sturdy, making them less prone to experiencing health issues. This makes them live long, up to ten to fifteen years in most cases.

- **This dog breed steps with a spring literally** – It is also natural for the Havanese to have a bouncy gait. It is one of those features that make the breed unique. This dog even has the ability to hop.

Deciding to own a Havanese will surely make you realize that there are so many cool things about this breed that you will love. What is even better about this breed is that it is unique. They have plenty of distinctive qualities that make them all the more adorable to their owners or masters.

Chapter 2 – Pros and Cons of Owning a Havanese Dog

Just like what has been indicated in the previous chapter, the Havanese dog makes for an adorable and amazing pet. This breed serves as a dedicated companion dog, which captures the interest of dog lovers not only because of the breed's adorable look but also because of its bubbly character. These cute dogs are also friendly and sociable. They are capable of making friends with everyone plus it is easy for them to get along with kids and other pets.

Top Reasons to Own a Havanese

If you are still deciding whether this breed is the most suitable choice for you, then here are some incredible reasons why taking home this breed can give you utmost satisfaction.

Naturally cheerful

One great reason why owning a Havanese is such an incredible decision is that it allows you to be with a dog who is naturally happy and cheerful. Imagine coming home with a happy and cheerful dog waiting for you and welcoming you at the entrance. It will surely let you imbibe positivity after a long and tough day. This breed will surely cheer you up. Every time you look at him, you will also feel good and happy about yourself. With the energy supplied by this dog, you can also squeeze some more energy from yourself, giving you the push that you need to spend more time every day playing with him.

Smart and intelligent

The Havanese is also one of the smartest dogs you can find at present. His high level of intelligence is one reason why you can easily train him. You can train your dog not only as a source of entertainment for yourself but also as a means of making yourself feel good and happy. You may experience that happiness and fulfillment especially after you notice this dog learning and improving under your supervision and care. As a smart and highly trainable dog, you will surely love seeing him grow and learning and mastering a few important tricks and commands.

Serves as a small pet

Another reason that will surely make you think about finally owning a Havanese is his small size. He is adorably small, which makes him truly beneficial in the modern world. His size is also a huge advantage especially if you just have a small living space, like an apartment. Since he is small, he will not need plenty of space to live and thrive. It is also more practical to own a tiny dog breed. If you want to have an idea about this breed's size, then take note that it usually goes around ten to eleven inches. With that, you are sure that this puppy can live and adapt well even in small spaces, like apartments and small houses. This is another good reason if you want to own a dog but have no budget to purchase a huge house yet. You can play and have fun with this breed even if you only have a small and compact space.

Gentle and easygoing

The gentle and easygoing personality of the Havanese also makes them incredible house pets. This specific personality is another reason why many dog lovers choose this breed. As a dog with a gentle personality, you can expect the Havanese to be perfect companions not only for kids but also for other animals. They can easily get along with children as well as other cats, dogs, and animals.

Highly sociable

You should also consider getting a Havanese because of their highly sociable nature. This means that they love to be with people. Expect to have plenty of snuggle times with him since he loves to stay with his owner. He will stick with you whenever he likes. The fact that he is exceptionally people-oriented may also cause him to tag along with you whenever you need to go out for quick errands. He will come with you even if you just put him in his carrying bag so he can ride next to you or let him sit in a carrier.

Positively responds to training

If you want a dog who responds well to all forms of training, then you can never go wrong by choosing a Havanese. You can easily motivate him with foods and treats.

There are times when he will display a streak of independence, causing his personality to become aloof, but you can expect that to change by providing him with a few tricks so he can begin to learn.

This breed often responds well to and excels in obedience and agility training. The reason is that the Havanese is highly intelligent. Moreover, he tends to be strongly motivated whenever he sees rewards.

Remains physically fit even with little to moderate exercise or activity

You will also love the fact that the Havanese does not require as much exercise and activities as the larger dog breeds. As a toy breed, they only need minimal and moderate levels of exercise to make themselves physically fit and healthy. As a puppy, you just have to take him for one to two daily walks and a bit of playtime at home or in your backyard. This should be enough to meet his daily energy requirements.

Displays coat markings that adhere to breed standard

The Havanese has several colors and markings that form part of their coat. The good thing about these markings is that they are part of the Havanese breed's standards, which is good if you intend to show that you own a purebred dog.

Some of the puppies you can find are those with cream markings, white marks, silver points or streaks, and Irish pied. These colors and markings will depend on the coat's overall color. Also, you will notice the Havanese holding standard colors, like chocolate, cream, red brindle, gold, and black.

Capable of following your mood

Another thing that makes the Havanese so lovable is their emotionally sensitive nature. It is the trait that makes them capable of taking on whatever your mood for the day is. The fact that they are among those dogs who are eager to please will make your own Havanese a truly great companion.

For instance, if he notices that you have a playful mood, then he will most likely play with you, too. If you want to walk, then expect him to be with you. In case you feel sick or just want to lie down and chill for a while, then he will do it with you. He can even comfort you whenever you feel down. What more can you ask for from a pet?

Are There Downsides to Owning a Havanese Breed?

While owning a Havanese seems to be an exciting prospect for dog lovers like you, remember that you can't expect everything to be perfect. There are still a couple of downsides and flaws that you have to prepare for, including the following:

- **Prone to developing anxiety** – Since Havanese is a small dog, he is at risk of developing anxiety. Note that he may overcompensate his small size through noise and stature, which is his way of announcing his presence. In other words, despite being small, there are instances when he can be obnoxious or loud. It can happen particularly when he is playing or whenever he feels like a threat is somewhere.

The Havanese is also afraid of being alone, which makes them prone to developing anxiety issues. This part of the breed's personality is something you have to consider before bringing one home. Note that leaving him at home for a long period may cause him to display destructive behaviors, like scratching and chewing.

Those are their ways of soothing themselves. It is also possible for them to vent out their frustrations by barking often. Fortunately, there are ways to handle these issues and soothe your puppy's separation anxiety. We will cover those methods in one chapter of this book so you will be able to gather clear and effective tips in handling his destructive behaviors, especially his separation anxiety.

- **Not that easy to housebreak** – Generally, the Havanese dog breed is easy to train. However, many of those who own one still say that the most challenging aspect during the training process is housebreaking. The primary reason why this is so is the size of the breed. His size makes it harder for him to recognize the fact that he has to go outside.

With that, you have to find out first if you have enough patience to housebreak this breed before you bring one home. Make sure to store some puppy pads once he is already with you.

Lay these pads out somewhere. This will serve as an encouragement for him to go in just one area of your home, instead of anywhere.

- **Displays mild stubbornness** – You should also know that some Havanese dogs are mildly stubborn. They often display this behavior whenever you stop playing with him or every time you take him home after your scheduled walk. They are among those dogs who want to expend all their energy by doing their favorite activities, so you may have a difficult time making your dog stop whenever he is enjoying his time doing something.

  This kind of stubbornness, however, is often noticeable in dogs who have to fend themselves rather than depending on a family to get the care and attention they need. With that said, you can prevent getting a Havanese with a stubborn nature by choosing to raise him while he is still a puppy.

Basically, these downsides are easy to deal with just by learning everything you can about the breed. Also, the benefits of owning a Havanese somehow outweigh the downsides, so getting this pet for yourself is definitely a wise decision. Just visit this pros and cons section every now and then so you can completely prepare yourself for his arrival and know exactly what to expect from him once you let him join your family.

Chapter 3 – Physical Attributes and Temperament

As a toy dog breed, the Havanese is kind of small. They are very adorable, though. They look great, which is the reason why many love this breed. You can expect a dog under this breed to grow around 8 to 11 inches. Your Havanese can also weigh around 7 to 13 pounds.

Despite the breed's small size, it is not so fragile. As a matter of fact, the Havanese is one of the most intelligent and active dogs you can find. Let's get to know more about this breed, especially in terms of physical attributes and temperament in this chapter. By learning about these areas of the Havanese, you will know exactly what to expect from him and do the necessary preparations before he ever reaches your home.

General Physical Features

Generally, you can see the Havanese as a sturdy and small-sized dog, which also boasts of his immense charm. This is a bit longer than a tall dog and has a long and untrimmed double coat. He has short legs combined with a long body and a friendly round-shaped face.

Another physical trait of this dog is the long-plumed tail, which tends to curl over his back. Some also consider his gait as a striking physical trait as it is noticeably bouncy and kind of playful. His springy gait is also what makes this breed distinctive when compared to the other breeds.

The Havanese is also easily distinguishable with his flat topmost skull. He also has a rounded back and a full muzzle, which tapers a bit at his nose. As for the eyes, the color is often dark brown and shaped like almonds. His eyes can immediately show how smart he is.

The Havanese also has a pair of ears that tend to arc a bit upward starting from the base then hang down both sides of his head. You can see these ears hanging down without touching the face.

Body

In terms of his body features, one thing you will instantly notice is the medium-sized neck, which is arched a bit. This medium-length neck bends smoothly to the dog's shoulder. He also has a quite prominent prosternum. As for his chest, you can see a slight depth and impressive muscles. You will also notice his well-sprung ribs as well as his tail, which has silky and long hair, that is being set quite high.

Hindquarters and forequarters

The Havanese also takes pride in his well-muscled hind legs that also feature moderate angulation. It has a higher croup compared to his withers. You will also notice his nails and pads that can come in any color.

In terms of the forequarters, you can see the topmost part of his shoulder lying at the withers. This specific position makes it possible for the next one to have a smooth and convenient experience whenever you decide to move on the back. There is also a shoulder layback, which helps in holding his head and neck high.

The forelegs are also impressive as they look straight regardless of what specific angle you view them from. You will also notice that the length from elbows to withers is similar to the one from the foot to the elbow. This breed also has feet with arched toes.

The Coat

The coat is the most interesting physical feature of the Havanese. It is soft and long while being lightweight, silky, and thick. The coat is also kind of wavy. It has a wide range of colors, including black and tan, gray, sable, black, and white. You can also see some of this breed having a mix of several colors and markings.

He has an inner coat, which is lighter compared to the exterior coat. One way to check whether his coat is truly good is to find out when you can see natural lines. If those appear, then the coat is indeed a good one, making the Havanese worthwhile to take home.

Another fact about the coat of the Havanese you have to be aware of is that it has a soft texture. Note, however, that this texture is more noticeable when he is still a puppy instead of when he reaches adulthood. One more thing about the Havanese is that it features corded coats, those that separate naturally to wavy parts and develop cords in young pets.

Temperament and Behaviors

The temperament of the Havanese is generally nice, thanks to his friendly and playful, as well as non-quarrelsome disposition. He is playful and alert, too. With this kind of temperament, it is safe to say that it is indeed a fantastic option for those searching for a family dog. His high level of energy makes him a source of entertainment for the entire family.

Havanese is also a generally happy breed, which is why you will notice him enjoying fun times playing with kids. He would love it if you take him out for daily walks. The good thing about the Havanese is that his energy is just enough, which means that it is not too overwhelming to put up with it.

However, some dogs under this breed are also quite shy, making it necessary to socialize them as early as possible. Another attribute about this breed you should keep in mind is that he gets attached to people closely, which is why he is also at risk of separation anxiety.

In that case, expect him to display some unwanted and destructive behaviors, like constant barking and chewing on your stuff. Fortunately, this is not that hard to fix. All it takes is to train him so he will know the difference between good and bad behaviors. If he barks too often, then you can fix it through training and by giving him a couple of physical and mental outlets designed to help lessen his barking tendencies.

Chapter 4 – Is the Havanese the Right Dog for You?

The Havanese is indeed one of the most adorable and the coolest dog breeds out there. They have a lot of great attributes that would encourage you to take one home and care for it. However, before you give yourself the go-signal, you should carefully weigh everything first. Find out if it is indeed the right breed for you; otherwise, you and the dog will end up having a bad experience.

When trying to find out whether the adorable Havanese is the perfect breed for you, ask yourself if you can provide him with everything that he needs. Among those that you should be able to provide this breed willingly are the following:

- **Someone who stays at home with him for the most parts of the day** – Remember that the Havanese does not want to stay alone, so he may not like it if you leave him on his own most of the time. There should be someone who will stay with him just in case you are not around.

- **A fenced yard** – It should not be an underground or electronic fence. It should help keep him safe.

- **Enough exercise once he matures** – Upon maturity, you should be able to provide your Havanese with adequate continuous exercise. Note that he needs adequate exercise to maintain a healthy weight. It is also necessary in draining all his energy, thereby ensuring that he will have a satisfying sleep at night.

- **Good grooming** – You should be able to spend some time grooming him. In this case, you should be ready to do a lot of brushing as well as some clipping or trimming of nails every few months.

- **Mental exercises** – Your Havanese will also need some form of mental stimulation constantly. With that, you should be capable of providing him with fun and interesting mental activities and exercises. He should also be able to play fun sports, like rally obedience, agility, and musical freestyle activity. He also needs to have access to challenging toys mainly designed for dogs.

- **Indoor lifestyle** – Another thing you have to assess before owning a Havanese is whether you can provide him with a good indoor lifestyle. He should love staying indoors because of the things you can provide to him inside – that is except, of course, when he needs to do bathroom breaks and exercise.

- **A healthy diet** – It should preferably be meat-heavy. You can go for either commercial or homemade ones, but since meat is undeniably costly, you have to ask yourself first if you can set aside a budget for healthy meat-based meals.

- **A budget for health emergencies** – Speaking of budget, you also need to find out whether you can set aside enough money for any health problem or emergency that your Havanese may encounter anytime. It also helps if you can get pet health insurance for him.

- **Sufficient time for housebreaking** – Note that the Havanese takes a while to housebreak, so you have to determine if you have a lot of time in your hands to dedicate to this training.

Apart from the ones mentioned, ask yourself whether you can also commit to giving him a thorough and fun socialization experience. Find out whether you have time and energy to introduce him to other animals and people. Keep in mind that even if the Havanese is often gentle and peaceful with others (whether other pets or humans), there are still several instances when they are conservative in front of strangers.

You need to have enough time to train him to socialize, so you can help him cultivate a more outgoing and confident personality and temperament. With that, you can prevent him from growing into an excessively timid and cautious dog.

It is also necessary for you to determine if you are indeed capable of becoming a responsible dog owner. Assess your capability and level of commitment. Remember that owning any dog, not just the Havanese, requires time, money, effort, and hard work, so you need to know if you are ready.

In that case, do a self-reflection on whether or not you will be a responsible dog owner by asking yourself the following questions and honestly answering them:

- *What are your real reasons for wanting a dog?* – Make sure that your reasons truly involve you. It should be what you want exactly. For instance, it would not be a wise idea if you only buy one to grant the request of your kids. You may regret your decision in the end since you do not wholeheartedly desire to own one.

- *Can you spend time with your dog?* – Note that just like other dog breeds, the Havanese requires your time and attention. You can't just ignore him because you had a stressful or tiring day. It is crucial for you to dedicate a lot of your time feeding, exercising, caring for, and bonding with him every day. With that, honestly reflect on your capability to give him time.

- *Can you afford the needs of your Havanese?* – One thing to remember about owning a dog is that it can get quite expensive. There are many things you have to pay for, including licenses, veterinary care, food, toys, grooming, and training classes. Find out if you truly have the money to support his needs in the long run.

- *Are you ready to handle specific problems caused by the dog?* – If you have breakable and special items at home, then you have to be all the more ready as these pets may cause

31

accidents, like breaking them. You should be completely ready to deal with accidents from the Havanese who is still not housetrained or one who became stressed and anxious upon reaching your home.

- *Are you living in a place that allows pets?* – If you are renting, for instance, make sure to find out whether pets are allowed first. Some communities set restrictions regarding pet ownership. You should be aware of all these before you decide to spend money on a Havanese.

- *Is your present living arrangement ideal for the dog?* – Research about the Havanese breed first, so you will know if this is the one that perfectly suits your present lifestyle and living arrangements.

- *Is there someone whom you can designate to take care of your Havanese if you are on a vacation?* – It is crucial to ask yourself if you can trust someone, a friend, neighbor, or relative, just in case you have to leave home for a few days for a business trip or to travel. Note that the Havanese needs to have a companion all the time, so you need to have a plan in place for these scenarios.

- *Are you willing to take responsibility for everything regarding your dog?* – Reflect on your ability to become a responsible dog owner. Note that there will be a lot of responsibilities you have to shoulder. You will have to commit to obeying the leash and licensing laws in your community.

Other responsibilities include providing your dog with identification tags, as well as a healthy diet, exercise, companionship, and love. You will also be responsible for bringing him to the vet regularly. Ensure that you are up for all these tasks before buying a Havanese.

All these questions and self-reflection will let you know if you are indeed fully prepared to take care of the dog his entire life. Moreover, you need to be committed and dedicated to building the appropriate leader and follower relationship with him. You should be capable of establishing yourself as a leader or master – someone that your Havanese will surely listen to and follow.

Also, find out whether there are signs that the breed is not compatible with you. A Havanese may not be the right fit for you if you dread dealing with:

- Separation anxiety, as well as excessive barking and destructiveness, especially if you leave him alone for prolonged periods

- Shyness particularly when he is lacking in proper socialization

- Mild stubbornness

- Barking tendencies

- Housebreaking challenges and difficulties

- Frequent combing and brushing

One thing to remember, though, is that the temperament that a Havanese inherited from his parents is not as predictable as the physical attributes, like shedding tendencies and size, he inherited. Despite having a natural and genetic behavior and temperament, you still have an assurance that you can shape this breed through proper training.

If you prefer to get a Havanese that does not have most of the breed's negative traits, then you may consider getting an adult one from a rescue group or animal shelter. By choosing an adult dog, it would be easy for you to assess right away what you will be getting. You can also easily determine which ones among the adult Havanese dogs you are eyeing have the best behaviors and traits.

If you prefer a puppy, though, then you can avoid the negative attributes and behaviors by dealing with the most reputable breeder. Find a good breeder who can provide you with the most appropriate and well-mannered Havanese puppy. You can find such a reliable breeder with the help of the guidelines and tips indicated in the next chapter of this book.

Chapter 5 - How to Find the Most Reliable Breeder?

Just like when searching for other purebred puppies, it is also crucial for you to dedicate a significant amount of your time to finding the most reliable breeder for your Havanese. Keep in mind that the majority of the Havanese dogs who are not in Cuba came from just eleven dogs, so you have to make sure that the breeder whom you intend to adopt or buy the puppy from takes really good care of it. A vital aspect of searching for the perfect Havanese for you is to look for a breeder who genuinely cares about the puppy. You have to search for a breeder who puts a lot of care into finding the perfect parents for the puppies under them.

One sign that you are dealing with a potentially good breeder is if they spend time talking to you regarding the adoption process, the things you should expect from the canine, as well as some pieces of advice once you successfully brought the puppy home. This shows that they genuinely care for the dogs that are under their wings.

Also, during your search for a reliable breeder, you will most likely encounter three types of them, namely the reputable, the puppy mill or disreputable, and the backyard breeder. You can expect these three to have major differences. You can also find two other kinds of breeders that are frequently lumped in any of the mentioned categories. These are the hobby breeders who are quite the same as backyard breeders and commercial breeders who refer to puppy mills.

So here are the things that you should know about the three breeders:

- **Reputable breeder** – This type mainly directs their effort to the Havanese breed's overall health and development. In most cases, a litter of Havanese puppies requires more cost and effort from a reputable breeder. As a matter of fact, the amount and effort they spent on the breed are usually more than what they earn from selling. It could be because of the numerous costs linked to breeding, as well as taking care of the breed, medical care and screening, proper and premium nutrition, and maintaining their healthy lifestyle.

  Some of the responsible and reputable breeders sell Havanese puppies at higher prices as a means of covering their legitimate breeding expenses. This is also their way of screening potential buyers so they can get an idea who among them can truly afford to provide the new pup with proper care.

  Breeders, who require the drawing of a purchase contract that features a health guarantee, spay and neuter clause, and a mutual agreement to bring back the Havanese to the breeder just in case you feel like you will no longer be able to care for him, are also among the most reliable ones.

You may need to spend more when buying your first Havanese from these reputable breeders. The process may also be a bit more complicated and costly than backyard and puppy mill breeders, but you have an assurance that it is all worth it since you have a lower chance of experiencing a problem later on.

- **Puppy mill breeder** – Another type of breeder that may offer you your first-ever Havanese is the puppy mill. The focus of this type is primarily on doing mass puppy production to earn a profit. They offer their dogs at low prices, but you should try to avoid them as much as possible. The reason is that they often put the dogs in inhumane and unsanitary conditions while offering the least veterinary care.

  In some cases, they sell the Havanese at an extremely high price so they can earn a huge profit even if the actual puppy is in poor health. Most of them are also lax when it comes to screening potential buyers of the puppy. Considering all the facts mentioned, it is advisable to avoid buying your first Havanese from a puppy mill.

- **Backyard breeder** – You may also encounter a backyard breeder in your search for someone who can provide you with the best Havanese dog. This type often has the qualities of both the puppy mill and the reputable breeder. You will notice most of them breeding their

Havanese to earn money while also doing it for their love and care to dogs.

The problem is that most of the backyard breeders in the market today do not have the necessary education and sufficient funds to breed a healthy set of Havanese puppies in the same way as to how a reliable and legitimate breeder can do it.

Since these breeders have the quality of both the puppy mill and the reputable ones, you can also expect some of them to be incapable of providing safe and sanitary living environments for the Havanese. Even though they love dogs and are genuinely fond of these pets, they also do the breeding mainly for money or income, so you have to be extra careful.

While you can choose to buy your first Havanese from any of the three types, it is still best for you to go for the first one – the reputable breeder. It will assure you that the Havanese you will be getting is of top-notch quality – one who is in the best health. To get in touch with a truly reputable breeder, here are some tips that should help you during the selection process:

Visit the breeder personally

If you want to assess how reliable a particular breeder is, you may want to visit him personally. Aside from giving you the chance to see how adorable and cute the Havanese puppies are, you will also have a closer look at how the breeder talks to his clients and cares for the dogs under their care. With that, you will surely have an idea if the breeder is indeed worthy to trust. Head to a local breeder offering the Havanese breed so you can see the puppies up close and personal. If you can't go there personally due to certain reasons, like the Covid-19 pandemic, you may want to communicate with the local breeder through Skype or video conferencing.

The goal here is to observe not only the breeder but also the dogs under their care. Find out whether the place is clean and whether or not the breeder is enthusiastic whenever he talks about and cares for his dogs. A personal visit will also give you an idea about whether or not the dogs are well-fed and the way they interact with the breeders and strangers. You will know that you are in the right place if the puppies and dogs there get along even with strangers.

Your visit to the breeder should also involve touring the kennels of both the puppy and his parents. The breeder should be willing to give you that tour. In that case, you should carefully check and observe the grounds. Find out if the grounds are clean and have odorless and clean exercise areas and kennels, too. It is also crucial to note that puppies do not have to be caged for quite a long time.

Your visit should give you a clear idea about the reputation and reliability of the Havanese breeder. Apart from closely examining the Havanese puppies you have to choose from, you will also be able to check their individual demeanor. Note that there may be puppies in there that walk with a bit of bounce. It is often based on their age. Your visit will also give you a closer look at all your options, giving you the chance to pick one that perfectly suits you.

Ask relevant questions

Make sure that you ask the breeder a lot of relevant questions, particularly those that can impact the life of the puppy you are eyeing to buy. Some of the most important and relevant questions you have to ask the breeder are the following:

- *What are the negative and positive attributes/qualities of the puppy's parents?* – Note that just like humans, the parents of the puppy can also greatly influence his personality. This information is crucial in determining what you can expect from the puppy exactly.

- *What kind of environment is he raised in?* – Find out whether he already underwent socialization training. It would be much better if the Havanese was raised and taken care of at home. This will familiarize him with the usual sounds in the household, including household appliances, like the vacuum cleaner and dishwasher.

With that, it will not be too challenging and difficult for you to familiarize him with his new environment. Also, it would be best if the puppy is already socialized so there will be no problems when he starts coming in contact with new and unfamiliar people and animals.

- *Is there a congenital defect?* – The breeder should also be able to provide you with information about any congenital defect affecting the puppy. This information is crucial as it will let you know if these defects will become a problem later on.

- *How does the breeder deal with health issues and illnesses developed by the dog once you have already purchased him?* – As a means of protection, ask about the plan of the breeder whenever your dog develops some health issues after your purchase. There should be a written agreement and formal contract signed by both of you so you will know what to expect when such an untoward event happens.

- *What are the required health certifications and tests that are already completed for each puppy?* – One section in this chapter will talk about the most important health certifications and tests, so you will have an idea about the most important ones that the puppy should go through right from the breeder before the ownership gets transferred to the buyer.

Ask the breeder if all these tests and certifications about the puppy's health are completed. If not, then it may be a good idea to find another breeder. Keep in mind that a good and reputable one is someone who has covered all the major points of the puppy's health. The breeder should also be able to provide a guarantee even for the most harmful issues related to genetics.

- *Will you take care of the puppy's initial health requirements?* – Note that another thing that a good breeder should do is to handle all the initial health requirements of the puppy. This should cover his first weeks and months, more specifically the shots. Also, remember that the Havanese, just like other puppies, need to go through specific procedures before leaving the mother's side. This is the key to ensuring that he will be healthy once you bring him home.

  Deworming and vaccinations also need to begin at around six weeks right after the puppy is born. It is important to continue these procedures every three weeks or so. You have an assurance that the puppy is old enough for his new fur parent to take him home if he has gone through most, if not all, of the required procedures. He should have completed the first stages of his most crucial healthcare requirements.

- *Does the Havanese need to be neutered or spayed before a specific age?* – If that is the case, then the breeder may ask you to sign a contract stating the need to perform the procedure under your care once the dog reaches a particular age. You have to carefully plan this procedure and do it in the best interest of your puppy.

- *Are you part of a legitimate Havanese group or organization?* – One sign that you are dealing with a truly good breeder is if it is part of a recognized group or organization that mainly focuses on the Havanese breed. Havanese Club of America is one of the most well-renowned groups that a good breeder may be a part of.

  Take note, though, that since these groups only got popular recently, you can't find that many of them. Despite that, you have an assurance that a breeder who is part of any of the legitimate Havanese groups or organizations out there is worth the trust. It somehow proves that the breeder offers nothing but the best to aspiring owners of Havanese dogs.

Mentioned are just a few of the many questions you should ask a particular breeder before you put your full trust in him. The goal here is to learn more about the dogs raised and cared for by the breeder, so you will be able to figure out if all of them truly receive what they need. This can also eliminate any issues in case you get a Havanese from an unreputable breeder who does not meet your standards and requirements.

Inquire about the early or initial stages of the Havanese life

The level of reliability of a specific breeder can also be assessed based on how they answer your inquiry regarding a particular Havanese puppy's initial or early life stages. The answers should revolve around how the breeder intends to provide the puppy with proper care and attention during his first few months.

You can immediately say that a breeder is reputable if he is willing to provide detailed information about such stages without sounding irritated nor annoyed that you are interested in such details. The information you will gather here will be extremely important in determining the amount and level of training the Havanese will undergo under the breeder's hands before you finally get a hold of one.

With that, you will also be able to develop the most appropriate plan that can help you successfully take over the puppy as soon as he arrives. If possible, go for a breeder who is willing to start with house training. It can contribute a lot to having a smooth-sailing experience once you take your puppy home since you can avoid the usual challenges linked to housebreaking or house training a Havanese.

Check reviews online

You will also get an idea regarding how good the reputation of a particular breeder is by spending time checking out online reviews. Some breeders actually make it a point to change their business name, especially those who received complaints online. However, if you try to search for their personal names together with the word Havanese in your search bar, then you have a higher chance of accessing some complaints raised against them.

You may also want to add the city you are in to your search term, so you will have a more targeted result. While you may be unable to access positive reviews since most of them are already posted on the site of the breeder, you can still determine if many prospective and existing dog owners already have a bad experience with them. The reason is that your targeted search terms may provide you with results that cover those who have horrible experiences with a specific breeder.

Conduct extensive research about your options

Upon deciding to own a new Havanese dog, some of the aspiring pet owners frequently want to get a hold of one right away. You should avoid this mistake. Avoid rushing your search for a Havanese as doing so may only cause you to purchase those dogs offered by puppy mills and backyard breeders. The fact that most of these breeders are unlicensed and unregistered means that you have no assurance about the quality of the puppies they offer. Most of them do not even provide proper socialization training and medical care to their dogs.

With that said, it is crucial to dedicate a lot of your time conducting research about different breeders. Find out which one breeds their dogs with good genetics. You have an assurance that a breeder is reputable enough if your research gives you results that they are indeed putting the health of their dogs on top of their priorities and ensure that these canines receive a proper diet.

Learn more about the parents, medical history, and age of the puppy

Ensure that the breeder is also willing to provide you with accurate information about the puppy's parents, his medical history, and actual age. Your knowledge about his parents is essential in determining the manner through which the dog will most likely grow. It is also the key to understanding his temperament, size, and appearance as he grows older.

You should also be able to get a hold of the puppy's complete medical history. There is a high chance that a Havanese breeder is worth putting your trust in if he is genuinely willing to provide and show proof about the medical screenings and certifications that the puppy went through.

The medical history that should be in your hands needs to be complete. In other words, there should be clear explanations regarding any medical condition he has and had. With the full medical history that you acquired from a reputable breeder, you will know exactly what you need to watch out for from the moment your puppy reaches your home. Make sure that you also get accurate information regarding the real age of the puppy. Note that a reputable Havanese breeder is one who will never let the puppies under their care leave before 10 to 12 weeks. You have to keep this detail in mind if you intend to deal with a truly reliable and trustworthy one.

Attend dog shows and ask for references and referrals

You also have a much better chance of keeping in touch with a good and reputable breeder if you regularly attend dog shows. Note that most of those dogs that are bred well are featured in a lot of dog shows. With that said, taking part in these events is definitely an incredible way for you to connect with like-minded people and get referrals from them regarding high-quality breeders.

There are also instances when you can ask for references from other reliable breeders. Most of them have several connections and amazing references, and you can expect them to provide you such info willingly during your search. Aside from that, you can seek referrals from a veterinarian. Your friends and loved ones can also be part of your ultimate sources of information when it comes to searching for a reputable breeder.

Be wary of red flags

As mentioned earlier, there are several breeders out there who claim to give you nothing but the best Havanese but only end up failing to fulfill what they promise. With that, you have to watch out for red flags that tend to let you know right away if the breeder is not that reputable. Among the red flags to observe from the time you are still searching for a breeder to the moment you do the personal visit and inspection are the following:

- Does not let you visit the Havanese puppy or dog prior to the purchase

- Has a strong and foul smell in the potty area – The area often has traces of urine or feces after the visit. The breeder may also be an irresponsible one if you notice the puppy having urine or feces on his fur or feet every time you get the chance to visit.

- Incapable of providing health clearances from the parents

- Discharge in the nose, mouth, and eyes of puppies

- Lethargy without any sign of curiosity and playfulness

- Makes puppies instantly available without requiring you to go through the waiting list

- Eager to sell their puppies on a license with complete ownership without adding a clause regarding spaying or neutering

- Employs staff who has little to no knowledge regarding the Havanese

- Continuously breeds dogs even at an old age, instead of letting them retire after several years

- Refuses to give you the necessary papers regarding your puppy that were printed together with the AKC logo.

- Does not require you to wait for a Havanese to become available

- Does not have the parents on site every time you visit

- Has puppies who look shy and reluctant when approaching new people

- Can't provide an accurate genealogy of the dogs they are caring for

- Has huge availability of puppies every year – This means that they do not follow the required limits in breeding pets annually.

If you notice any of these red flags, then it may be an indication that you have to look for another breeder.

Assess the required health tests and certifications

One thing to note about the Havanese is that the breed has an extremely unique history. This uniqueness is what will probably cause him to experience a few genetic problems. If you want your puppy to receive proper and genuine care, then it is advisable to learn about the specific diseases you have to monitor and check upon.

You have to know the diseases you need to watch out for in the future, so you can give the puppy the right care. As a part of the initial examination, determine the health issues that may have been bugging the puppy's parents. In this case, the Havanese needs to undergo the following testing:

- Hip dysplasia evaluation

- Hypothyroidism

- Elbow dysplasia clearance

- Von Willebrand disease

- Thrombopathia

The puppy also needs to have his eyes examined by a legitimate and reliable ophthalmologist who also specializes in dogs. In terms of certifications, take note that the standards are not extremely strict. However, if the breeder you have chosen is a member of the Havanese Club of America, then this indicates the need to follow a set of standards to give you an assurance that the puppy, as well as his parents, are in best health and shape.

If the breeder you intend to deal with is a member of an organization that practices such standards, then they have to adhere to even the minimal set of requirements. Not meeting the requirements of the organization means that the breeder can't become a member. It somehow assures you that all the breeders belonging to the mentioned options and are members of the organizations are highly predictable and reliable in the manner they treat puppies.

Check the contracts and guarantees

Check the contracts and guarantees provided by the breeder before putting your full trust in them. These contracts and guarantees are around to protect both the puppy and the buyer. Spend time examining such papers, so you can receive full protection. Do not sign any contract without reading all the details indicated in it.

Also, ensure that you are genuinely willing to meet each requirement and standard indicated in the contract before putting your signature on it. In most cases, these contracts are easy to understand, so comprehending them won't be that huge of a problem.

The presence of a contract also indicates the desire of the breeder to protect the puppy that they will turn over to you as well as your interest. Some contracts will require you to agree on caring for the dog in a specific manner. This is actually a good thing as this means that the breeder wants to confirm whether you

51

are indeed serious about looking after the welfare of the dog.

A good contract also often includes policies regarding neutering and spaying once the Havanese puppy matures. There are instances when it will indicate the right of the breeder to retain the puppy's registration papers, though, you will still be given legit copies.

As for the guarantee, it will usually indicate the specific health conditions guaranteed by the breeder for each puppy under their care. In most cases, the guarantee will provide comprehensive details regarding the health of the dog as well as any recommendations on the specific steps that the new owner will have to undertake once he/she takes it home.

It is also in the guarantee where you can see schedules at the beginning of the puppy's health care, which was already accomplished by the breeder. This will serve as your guide on creating the proper schedule that you can refer to when continuing the puppy's health care routines. The guarantee should also state that you can return the puppy to the breeder just in case you discovered a severe health issue within a designated timeframe or period.

Aside from the contract's inclusions and guarantees, it should also indicate what is no longer under the scope of the breeder's care. This means that there should be clear information on what the breeder does not guarantee.

One thing to remember is that the guarantee is usually lengthy. As a matter of fact, it is often longer compared to the actual contract. Despite being long, you should read and understand it completely before inking your signature. That way, you will know exactly what you are getting into and what can you expect from the breeder.

Request for information regarding the puppy's parents

One sign that you are dealing with a reliable breeder is when they can easily and quickly provide you with information regarding the genetics or parents of the Havanese you are eyeing to buy. Note that the Havanese has a focused lineage, which means that the breeder can easily track its genetics. This is especially true for those who are also members of legitimate Havanese organizations.

It is crucial to gain first-hand information about the Havanese puppy's genetics as this will let you know what to expect from him. Spend time reviewing the history of his parents since doing such will give you an idea about what you should watch out for once he grows and ages. By gathering information about the puppy's genetics, you will have a much better idea of the way the puppy will behave based on the personality and habits of his parents.

Asking the breeder for this specific information is also the key to getting a feel on how they perceive the puppy. Keep in mind that you will most likely have several questions upon successfully reviewing the contract and the other paperwork. A good breeder can supply you with answers to your questions, especially regarding the parents. You will know that you are dealing with a good one if he can quickly provide a detailed, emotional, and comprehensive picture of the puppy's parents.

Observe whether the breeder asks you the right questions

When planning to communicate with a good breeder, remember that a sign that you are dealing with a genuinely trustworthy and responsible one is when they take time to interview future owners of the dogs they breed. Some of them will throw a lot of relevant questions regarding you, your habits, activities, and experiences, as well as your family, living situation, and the reasons for wanting to own this breed.

This particular interest in you shows that the breeder is truly after the welfare of their dogs. They want to be one hundred percent sure that the person they choose can provide their dogs with the right care and environment. It can also help them determine the specific puppy who perfectly suits you as they will take time in figuring out which one can adjust to your household and lifestyle.

In most cases, a trusted breeder will ask potential buyers and dog owners the following questions:

- What are your reasons for owning a puppy?

- Do you have experience with taking care of a puppy? Are you already adept when it comes to introducing and familiarizing a puppy to a new home or environment?

- Can you provide the health and veterinary care needs of the puppy?

- Can you commit to neutering or spaying the puppy and showing proof of it once he matures?

- Can you commit to training your puppy and letting him take part in obedience classes if possible?

- Do you already have a plan in place for your puppy in case you leave home for a few days for business or vacation?

- Where do you intend to make your puppy live – indoor or outdoor?

- Is there a fenced yard in your home? How do you intend to make your puppy exercise in case you don't have a fenced yard?

- Did you own a pet before? Are you taking care of another pet right now?

- Are you following a more active lifestyle? Or is it sedentary?

- Do you want the puppy you intend to buy to serve a certain purpose in your family or at home? Do you plan to train it for a certain purpose, like alert work, service work, or search and rescue?

- Can you commit to helping your puppy get adequate exercise every day?

- Are you familiar with the Havanese breed?

- Are you living in your own home or are you renting?

And so much more. The goal of the breeder for asking you such questions is to assess your capabilities and commitment when it comes to providing only the best for the Havanese puppy you plan to take home. If the particular breeder you are communicating asks you such questions, then there is a high chance that they are excellent providers of dogs as their focus is on the welfare of the breed and the interest of both parties.

Other Signs that You are Dealing with a Good Breeder

You can also assess the legitimacy and trustworthiness of your chosen breeder based on a number of signs. Here are other signs that will let you know immediately whether the breeder deserves your trust:

- Encourages regular visits to the new puppy before you officially bring him home

- Requires or requests your entire family to visit and meet the puppy before taking him home

- Has puppies and dogs on site that are completely healthy – with bright eyes and normal levels of energy

- Does not force you to work with a certain veterinarian – The breeder is okay with the veterinarian you choose provided he/she is a licensed and reliable one.

- Requires signing of a puppy contract with a neuter/spay clause – There should also be a clause for "return to breeder" in case you will be unable to take care of the puppy.

- Has a true waiting list for the dogs and puppies under their care

- Does not agree on shipping or selling puppies without the buyer/s seeing them personally first

- Offers real copies of health clearance certifications for the Havanese's parents

- Provides a health guarantee for each puppy

- Sticks to a limited number of breeding frequency annually – This means that the breeder only breeds a certain number of puppies every year.

- Does not breed a dog breed over four times annually

- Provides complete genealogy details of both parents

- Has sanitary and clean-living quarters for puppies and dogs

- Boasts of well-groomed and clean dogs when you visit them on site – The dogs should be free from fur, feces, urine, or any stain, especially on their legs, belly, and feet. The dogs and puppies also need to be properly groomed free of any mats in their fur.

- Has curious and healthy puppies – This means they are willing to learn more about you as well as the surroundings.

- Has healthy parents, even just one of them, on site – The breed's parents also need to have a great temperament

- Participates in organizations specific to the Havanese breed – The breeder should also take part in canine activities, such as flyball or agility

- Has more than enough knowledge regarding the Havanese – A good breeder will also eagerly listen and share his/her knowledge with you.

- Asks several questions not only about you but also regarding your family, as well as your reasons for owning one

By keeping everything you have learned from this chapter in mind, you can surely communicate with a trusted breeder. It will bring you closer to your goal of owning and taking care of the most intelligent and adorable Havanese.

Chapter 6 – Choosing the Right Havanese Puppy

Now that you know how to choose a reputable breeder, it is time to understand how you can pick the right Havanese puppy. Remember that your goal will always be to find a healthy Havanese – one who is active and has all the nice personalities typical of the breed. You do not want to end up with a sickly dog – one that shows signs that his breeder does not take good care of him.

Make sure that you are also aware of the actual cost you will probably spend for the Havanese as well as the specific factors that can affect it. That way, you can prepare for that amount and determine if it is indeed something you can handle and work with.

Making your Choice

Picking the right Havanese puppy is typically the same as when you are choosing one from other breeds. It will all boil down to what you want exactly as well as the things and features you want the dog to have. You may look at the whole experience as totally enjoyable and entertaining, but be prepared to deal with challenges and difficulties, too.

Yes, it is fun to choose a puppy, particularly if it is from the adorable Havanese breed. However, you have to be serious and extra careful to prevent yourself from being swayed by irrelevant things that may bother you in the future.

One thing that you have to do is to observe the puppies closely once you visit a particular breeder. Observe the ability of each puppy to play and interact with others – whether it is with other dogs or people. The results of your observation will let you assess the capability of the puppy to respond to other pets who may already be living with you at present.

Also, observe how the puppies interact as a pack. Find out if they display aggressiveness or mistrust. If that is the case, then avoid choosing one from such a pack. However, you also do not want to pick a puppy who seems too frightened of your presence. One sign that he is terrified in front of someone, especially a stranger, is when he tucks or shrinks his tail away all the time. Avoid a puppy who gets easily terrified or frightened as it may cause problems during the training at home.

Your goal should be to find a litter filled with friendly and lively puppies. You should be able to sense their friendly nature even those who seem to ignore you at first. Remember that it could be that he wants to play with his littermates first or determine the situation upon seeing you.

Also, observe whether a puppy from the pack seems to be so excited to meet you. A lot of dog owners often perceive it as an indication that such a puppy is the most suitable one for them and their family. However, remind yourself that this premise is not true all the time. Some puppies who seem to be too excited to meet and greet you right away are somewhat more demanding and forward than those who seem to look at you first to analyze what is happening.

Some seem afraid just because they want to completely comprehend the scenario first before getting themselves involved. In most cases, they are the tamed ones and they exhibit more patience than the others. You will also have an easier time training them. However, avoid one who does not come to you because he is obviously afraid and terrified of strangers.

One more tip when it comes to choosing a puppy is to look for one with the specific personality traits you intend to see. For instance, if you are interested in having a friendly, fun, and forward dog, then you can pick that who seems to greet you right away even if it is still the first time you meet. If the dog you want is one who reflects on things first, then choose the mellower one from the pack.

Should you Pick or Adopt an Older Dog?

Another thing you should do is to figure out whether an older Havanese is the more suitable option for you instead of a puppy. Going for an older Havanese may be the most suitable option for you, especially if you are not interested to spend a lot of your time and effort researching a reputable breeder and waiting for the puppy to grow while being hands-on with all the training that he has to go through.

Note that buying a Havanese puppy can be tiresome as missing just one to two days of training might cause you to go back to the beginning. An adult or mature Havanese is much easier to take care of. It is even okay for him to miss one to two days of training since he is already aware of the basics, particularly housetraining. Aside from that, bonding with and connecting to an adult Havanese also seems to be very satisfying. Aside from skipping the somewhat messy and frustrating training, which is a requirement for puppies, you will also feel good knowing that you provide a home to a deserving adult dog. It lets you save a dog who no longer has a place to go and needs a loving family who will take care of him. There is a high chance that an adult dog is the kind of companion you want and need since he will probably want to stay with you all the time, too.Another advantage of adopting an adult Havanese is that there is a possibility that he already mastered a few tricks and commands. You can explore what he already knows and begin a new training routine for him. It can be an extremely fantastic bonding moment, which will let him know how excited you are about spending a lot of time with him. You may also want to go for an adult Havanese if you want to begin your journey towards self-improvement. The reason is that he will be a great companion for reaching your goal. For instance, if you have been longing to incorporate a few minutes of exercise into your daily routines, then choosing an older dog will let you start with it right away. You will not be trapped at home teaching a puppy the basics since an adult one already knows them.

With that, you can begin your exercises that will also serve as your bonding session. Also, the good news is that there are numerous activities that will work for both of you. You can even expect the Havanese to join you in exploring new places.

Adopting an Adult Dog from a Havanese Rescue

You may want to visit a Havanese rescue if you intend to own an adult dog. It is also the most suitable place to get your dog, especially if you have plans of giving this pet a second chance rather than undergoing the lengthy process of working with a breeder.

The good thing about adopting from a rescue is that it is less expensive than having to buy a puppy who has just been born. The fact that the dog is already fully grown also means that he has mastered specific commands and has already been housebroken, at the very least.

Also, a lot of rescues specializing in saving dogs are now easy to access and find. However, keep in mind that if you plan to adopt a Havanese from any of these rescues, there is a high chance that you can't take one home. Most of the dogs are in these rescues because their previous owners failed to provide them with the time and care they need. It could be because of their financial incapacity or their failing health.

Other previous owners may also put their dogs on these rescues because they moved to a new place that does not permit pets.

Some were abused. Other dogs were abandoned by choice or circumstances. With that said, it is highly likely for Havanese rescues to be really vigilant and extra careful in selecting a new home for the dogs under their wings.

In that case, you have to prove that you are indeed capable of adopting any dog from a legitimate Havanese rescue. Fill out the necessary application forms that will indicate your willingness to adopt. Be willing to undergo a house inspection, too. Just be prepared as there is a chance for your application to be rejected as they will assess your living conditions as well as the details you have entered in your application.

Another thing you should remember is that not all Havanese rescue organizations are trustworthy. The reason is that you can't expect each one to be actual shelters specifically designed for the well-being of the canines. Note that there are several instances when people act like rescuers when the truth is, they operate puppy mills, passing off the pooches they have illegally homegrown as surrendered puppies then charging clients with fees that are higher than usual.

To prevent yourself from dealing with such fraudulent people, make sure that you inspect the place closely. Learn more about the volunteer service they are claiming to do prior to committing and supporting fraudulent ones unintentionally. One way to examine organizations and associations closely and spot whether they are a fraud is to visit them personally.

Ask the right questions, too. Among the questions you have to ask to determine if the one you are dealing with is trustworthy are:

- How did you obtain the Havanese rescue?

- Is there a reputable and dignified breeder, kennel, or dog club that highly recommends your organization?

- When did you start this business? Have you been in this industry for a long time already?

- What were your reasons for starting this program?

- Will you spend time assessing the suitability of a specific canine with a prospective owner?

- How do you use donations? Do you use it to support animals or do you spend a part of them for your staff?

Assess the reliability and legitimacy of a specific Havanese rescue based on the answers provided to you as you ask the questions.

Signs that You are Dealing with a Good Havanese Rescue

Apart from asking questions, it is also advisable to check whether the Havanese rescue you are visiting shows signs that they are indeed deserving of your trust. Some things that the Havanese rescue should do that immediately indicate that they are highly reputable are:

- Ensures that the dogs they rescued were already neutered and spayed before putting them up for adoption

- Guarantees the good health of their pets and updates vaccinations

- Provides an adoption contract stating the need to return the dog to the rescuer in case one needs to re-surrender it – The contract needs to be signed by both parties for it to be valid, too.

- Screens everyone who wants to adopt a Havanese – The organization should also have it in their policies to visit your home to ensure that it provides an ideal environment for the Havanese.

- Adheres to the limitations of their resources – They are fully aware of their limited resources, making them understand how important it is to avoid taking in or rescuing more dogs than what they can conveniently and legally care for and accommodate.

If your goal is to adopt a Havanese, then your main concern should be to look for a Havanese rescue who is capable of putting the welfare and the best interest of your future household companion on top of their priorities. Adopting a Havanese rescue is also your best bet if you genuinely prefer an older dog, instead of a puppy.

Chapter 7 – The Cost of Owning a Havanese Puppy

If you have decided to buy a Havanese puppy from a reputable source, be it from an actual breeder or from an animal shelter or Havanese rescue, then the actual purchase cost should be one of your considerations. On average, a purebred Havanese puppy costs approximately $1,000 to $1,500. It is kind of costly, though, it does not necessarily mean that you will have to pay more than a thousand dollars for this breed.

Depending on a few factors, you can make it go down to $700. However, there are also instances when the cost can soar up to $2,500. Several factors can indeed cause the price of this breed to go down or soar – chief of which is its overall quality. This means that Havanese puppies guaranteed to be of top-notch quality also have extremely high price tags.

Key Factors that Influence the Cost of a Havanese

For you to really know what to expect when you start shopping for a Havanese, you have to familiarize yourself with the specific factors that can either increase or decrease its final purchase price. Here are just a few of them:

Overall Quality

As mentioned earlier, the overall quality of the Havanese plays a crucial role in its final cost. You can expect the quality of the puppy to be determined based on his pedigree, genetics, as well as potential health issues. In most cases, you will spend more if you choose a purebred dog than a mixed breed.

The bloodline and genetic history of the puppy can also determine his overall quality. If a puppy comes from parents recognized as purebred show quality dogs bred by a well-renowned breeder, then expect the purchase price to be significantly high. The fact that it comes from a highly reputable breeder can also cause its price to soar as it means that more financial investment is made to ensure that the puppies and dogs are well taken care of.

One thing you should remember, though, is that apart from paying a higher amount for the purebred, you may also spend a lot on curing any health issues he may encounter later on. With that in mind, you really have to be extra cautious and wise when making your choice even if the ones introduced to you are purebred. Pick one with optimum health.

Age

Another factor that greatly affects the final purchase price of the Havanese is the actual age. For those who intend to buy this breed for competitions and shows, getting an adult one wouldn't be much of a problem. This is actually good if you want to spend less because older ones are cheaper than puppies. The main reason is the high demand for puppies.

As you can see, most of those who want to own a Havanese prefer a puppy who is around 5 to 8 weeks. The reason is that it is the perfect age to form a bond with the puppy. It also defines his formative years for feedback and training, among many others. With that said, the price of a puppy is unsurprisingly higher compared to adults.

As for the older ones, it is highly likely that they already went through training. Most of them were also vetted already. Others were bred for competitions and shows. In that case, they can cost high, though, it will still not be as pricey as a Havanese puppy.

Certification and registration papers

The main purpose of these certification and registration papers is to confirm the heritage and level of quality of a particular Havanese. It would be best if the registration papers have the terms AKC or CKC. It indicates that aside from the fact that you are dealing with a reliable and certified breeder, they also adhere to the rules and guidelines meant for the purebred.

These terms also prove that a particular breeder is a certified member of a legitimate kennel club. There are also instances when these breeders register their puppies and dog that may also influence the final price that the buyer has to pay.

If you plan to take home a Havanese from a rescue or shelter, then be aware that it also comes with papers. These papers often show the dog's medical history, admission date, and the certificates of both his parents.

Your knowledge about these things is actually very helpful when searching for a good household pet. It also provides relevant details about the potential ailments of the dog, his medication bills, and possible treatments.

Medical expenses and health screenings

The price of a Havanese will also most likely go up or down based on the medical expenses already incurred and the health screenings conducted. Keep in mind that a serious and reliable breeder often requires their puppies and dogs to undergo testing and evaluation for a wide range of health and medical conditions.

Some breeders also do regular vet visits to let their breeds undergo a medical exam, deworming, microchip implantation, and vaccination before they finally sell them. If that is the case with your chosen breeder, then expect the price to be higher than usual. The good news is that it is worth it as it also means that the puppy you will be getting has a lower risk of developing severe health issues.

Socialization and training

The final purchase price of a Havanese will also be affected by the socialization and training he already received from his breeder. One thing you should know about the majority of reliable breeders right now is that they only sell the dogs under their care after socializing and training them.

This kind of training increases the price of the puppy. Despite the high cost of a socialized and trained dog, it is still worth it since you can also save money in the long run. The reason is that you will not have to spend on his training once you take him home. It also lets you take home a well-behaved dog.

Location

The location also matters a lot in the final price. The cost of a Havanese puppy varies from one breeder to another based on the breed's popularity in your present location. For instance, since the Havanese is more like a small dog, you can expect the breed to be more famous in metropolitan locations. Those are the places where the majority of people live in tiny spaces.

If you are staying in such locations, then expect the price to be higher because of the great demand. If you want, you may compare the prices of Havanese from breeders in various locations. The problem is that buying a dog from a different location can be quite risky as it means you will not be able to meet the breeder and visit the kennel and the dogs personally.

Other Possible Expenses

The purchase price of the Havanese is not the only one you will be spending on. You will also have to prepare a certain amount for the things he needs once you bring him home. It is the reason why you have to ask yourself first whether you are indeed financially capable to provide this dog breed everything that he needs to live a healthy and happy life with you.

The following is a summary of other things you may have to spend on once you officially become the owner of the Havanese and take him home:

Primary supplies

Once you have officially purchased the puppy or the adult Havanese, you should prepare for his arrival. In that case, you need to gather several supplies so they will be ready during his scheduled arrival at your home. In most cases, you will be spending around $150 to $650 during the Havanese first year in your home. You may also need to spend around $55 to $260 annually on supplies after that first year. However, take note that this price may also differ based on your present location, the specific place where you shop the items, and the overall quality of your chosen products and supplies. To give you an idea of the things you have to spend on initially, here are some of the most common supplies (together with their average cost) that the Havanese use from the moment their new owners take them home:

- Water and food bowls $10
- Leash $10
- Dog collars $20
- ID tag $10
- Dog bed and crate $35
  and $40, respectively
- Popper scooper $20
- Plastic poop bags $55
- House training pads $25
- Dog toys $30
- Dog shampoo $10
- Brush $15
- First aid kit $30
- Odors and stains removal spray $10
- Toenail clippers $10
- Toothbrushing kit $10

Apart from the ones mentioned, you may also need to pay for additional supplies, such as a harness, anti-chew spray, door gate, yard fences, doggy playpen, a muzzle, and some dog clothes. If you want to save money on these supplies, then it would be best for you to visit second-hand stores and websites.

Training cost

During the course of caring for the Havanese, you will also need to spend on training. Keep in mind that this breed is easy to train because of its intelligence. With that said, it is not a requirement to let him undergo professional training.

However, it would still be better for you to let him go through some group lessons so he can learn basic obedience. It is also the key to socializing him. These lessons usually cost around $150 to $200 covering five sessions with each session often taking an hour.

Also, remember that even if the Havanese is easy to manage, you may still want to invest in a dog training book that you can consult anytime. The good thing about these training books is that they are not that expensive.

Just buy a dog training book or two before bringing home your Havanese so you will know the basics of training him. This will definitely help in establishing a harmonious relationship not only between you and your dog but also between him and your entire family.

Medical cost

You also have to set aside some funds for the medical costs of your Havanese. Note that the estimated medical costs for the Havanese breed are often around $385 to $795. This cost usually covers his first year. You will also need to pay around $280 to $645 annually after that. The cost may also differ depending on the experience of the vet as well as other factors, like the location, the present health of the dog, and the specific clinic that will take care of him. You should plan to spend around $50 to $300 for neutering and spaying. It is just a one-time expense so you do not have to worry about it taking a huge chunk of your budget. Several clinics will charge at least $100 for neutering and spaying, but you can also find other alternatives that support the successful performance of this procedure at a low cost, usually just $50. Generally, you can expect the spaying process for females to be costlier than the neutering process for males.

Veterinary cost

Another cost you have to seriously consider is that involving regular visits to the vet. It would be necessary for your dog to visit the vet regularly as this is the key to keeping him in tip-top shape. The first vet schedule should be when your Havanese is still around 8 weeks. It is crucial to prepare for each vet visit as it will cost you around $65 to $170. In most cases, it will cover crucial vaccines, physical and fecal examination, and the initial three doses for preventing flea and heartworm. It would also be best to let your dog take the heartworm and flea prevention for the remaining parts of the year. With that, you get the chance to prevent heartworm from developing. Your Havanese may also be required to take vaccines based on your activities and lifestyle. Some of the conditions that require the use of vaccine so your puppy will be completely protected from them are:

- **Lyme** – The vaccine for this may cost around $60 to $80. This cost already includes the booster shot. It is an ideal vaccine for your Havanese if he gets exposed to ticks frequently.

- **Leptospirosis** – You may need to spend around $15 to $25 for this vaccine. Your Havanese needs this to protect him from leptospirosis, especially if he is always exposed to standing water and wildlife or you take him on hiking or camping trips frequently.

- **Influenza** – Your dog also needs to be vaccinated for flu. This is even more important if the kennel or daycare your dog regularly visits recommend it because of intermittent flu outbreaks. This specific vaccine may require you to spend around $70 to $90.

Aside from the vaccines, there are also other medical expenses you have to spend for on the coming years. Annual visits to the vet can range from $125 to $265 that may cover the necessary vaccines, general exams, and heartworm tests. If the dog is older, then bloodwork may be necessary to spot possible hidden health issues. A fecal exam may also be necessary in case the quality of your dog's stool is somewhat inconsistent.

Dog insurance

It also helps if you set aside a budget for dog insurance. This is crucial especially because you will have a hard time predicting medical expenses. Request a quote from various pet insurance companies so you will know more about their offers and coverage. By providing your Havanese with dog insurance, you will be fully prepared regardless of the medical condition he is facing.

Remember that the Havanese is also prone to developing certain health conditions, like heart disorders. By investing in his insurance, you will have peace of mind knowing that you have enough funds to support his health.

Just make sure to compare various insurance policies, so you can pick one that truly has good coverage. In this case, consider certain factors, like the type of deductible (whether it is annually or per incident) as well as the amount, reimbursement limit and percentage, and the actual start of the coverage.

You also have to compare and check the included services in the coverage, like surgery, emergency visits, specialists, pre-existing conditions, medications, and hospitalization. Moreover, remember that the cost varies based on several factors, like the age of your Havanese, your chosen plan, and the location.

Food

Of course, you will also need to spend some money when feeding your Havanese. Note that an adult Havanese usually weighs an average of 10 lbs., so you can calculate food-related expenses after you comb through the prices of several bestselling brands.

In most cases, a Havanese puppy will consume almost 70 pounds of food, which may put the average cost for dog food during the first year he is with you at around $85. You can also expect adults to require a similar amount of food.

One thing to remember when shopping for dog food is that there is a noticeable gap in the prices of cheap and premium brands. The final price you will have to pay for the food also depends on your selected brand. You also have to include in your food budget some dog treats.

Now that you know the usual cost of buying your first Havanese, as well as the supplies and other expenses you may have to budget for, it is time to make the final decision of purchasing one. If you feel like you can afford to buy the Havanese and the expenses that come afterward, then you should contact your chosen breeder or Havanese rescue. Once you have finally picked a dog and paid for it, you should start preparing for his arrival.

Chapter 8 - What Do You Need for the Arrival of your Havanese?

Just like what has been indicated in the previous chapter, there are certain things that you have to invest in so you can completely prepare for your puppy's arrival. Determine what your Havanese needs exactly, especially during the time when he still tries to familiarize himself in his new environment. Some of the most important ones you should prepare before the scheduled arrival of your Havanese are the following:

Crate

You have flexible choices when it comes to a dog crate, but you have to make sure that you consult the breeder first and find out if the puppy has his own preferences. That way, you can meet what he wants. Also, it is advisable to pick the most appropriate size – one that is not too small nor too large for him. It should be enough that he can comfortably sleep and turn around.

An extremely small crate is not a good idea as it may limit his movements too much and make him feel lonely and isolated. Avoid an extremely large one, too, as this may only increase the risk of him soiling it. In terms of materials, you have a couple of choices – the plastic and the metal ones.

The plastic crate features diagonal walls that somehow limit the internal space. It also tends to let in only minimal light and consumes more space if you decide to travel with it. One major problem with this option is that it is easy for the Havanese to chew on it, which may break his teeth in the long run. It has nice doors and color varieties, though.

If you want a roomier option, then go for metal crates. This material allows a higher amount of light to penetrate. A metal-based crate is also collapsible, making it ideal for those who want to travel. It is heavier compared to the plastic crate, though, but it still looks nicer plus it lets you attach several things to it.

As for the size, most Havanese owners agree that their puppies feel more comfortable with a 21-inch crate. They also use this size until the time when their Havanese fully grows.

Playpen

Another thing that you may have to invest in for your Havanese is the playpen. Fortunately, it comes in various materials and sizes, so you can make a choice based on what you think is appropriate enough for your needs. One thing to note about the Havanese, though, is that they like to climb. Several of the new Havanese puppies even do it to get out of their playpens.

As a matter of fact, they can climb up to a height of 4 feet and they can do it even if they have just arrived in their new home. If you plan to buy a plastic playpen, then be aware that it has a smaller grid that will make it a lot easier for your puppy to climb on. Before making your final purchase, though, it is crucial to consider the following:

- Is there enough room for the potty pad?

- Will your puppy use a potty pad or will he start potty training outdoors right away?

- Is a playpen really necessary?

- What type of surface will you be putting the playpen on?

- Is it a good fit for your house?

A playpen is surely a valuable investment especially if you think about how it lets you play with your new pet without worrying about him escaping. It can make him feel at home somehow. It also contributes to preventing your puppy from being overwhelmed with his new environment, as well as when you are still training him to go potty.

Dog Collar/Harness

The dog collar or harness is an essential investment, especially once you start to take your puppy outdoors. Your pup's first few weeks will most likely be inside the home as well as in his pen, but it would be best for the dog collar or harness to be around, so you will be able to use it right away. You will find it useful every time you intend to bring your puppy outdoors to go potty or take him for his outdoor walk. It is also a big help during the training.

One thing you should remember about the Havanese puppy is that his neck is quite small, so you may find it challenging to find the best collar and harness that is small enough for him. Still, you have to look for a small collar – one that perfectly fits your Havanese puppy's small neck. You can identify the size that specifically fits him by measuring his chest area then consulting the suggested or recommended size of the manufacturer. Note that every manufacturer has its own measuring chart, so do not forget to use it as your guide. Measure the neck of your puppy, too. If you have no flexible measuring tape around, then a wise move would be measuring the neck using a string then measuring the string against a ruler. Leave sufficient space for two fingers to fit beneath the collar comfortably. Avoid leaving too much, though, as it may only cause you to buy a collar or harness that will catch your puppy's lower jaw or slip over his head.

When shopping for a collar, avoid picking one with cheap plastic buckles, too. The reason is that this material is prone to cracking. Also, avoid locking too tightly. You may also purchase a cat collar just in case you can't find one that is small enough for your puppy. If you got your puppy during his 9th to 13th week, then the best collar would be that, which is around six to nine inches long and three-eight inches thick.

Another thing to remember about the collar is that the thinner ones can lower the likelihood of it matting the hair of your Havanese. You can also go for leather collars, but make sure that you pick a rolled dog collar as it contributes to preventing mats.

Sherpa Bag

Any other brand of bag will also work, provided it is large enough to make the puppy feel comfortable. You will be using this item whenever you take your pup on a trip or visit the vet. You can even put your Havanese puppy in the bag so you can make him sleep beside you during the first few nights.

Towels or Washable Crate Pads

You can use any old absorbent towels you have at home and put them on the dog crate. If possible, put multiple layers of the towels and a waterproof pad between each of them. Alternatively, you can invest in washable crate pads – around two to three pieces. One of them for changing, another for washing, and the remaining one as a reserve.

Blanket

You also need to prepare a blanket. This should cover all sides of the crate. With this blanket covering the sides of the crate, your puppy will feel like he is in a den, significantly boosting his comfort level. You may also want to buy a crate cover or make one on your own.

In case you decide to use an x-pen, then you may still like the idea of putting a crate inside to let your puppy have a sleeping space, which can be transformed into a play yard soon enough.

Dog Tag

It is also advisable to shop for dog tags before you take a puppy home. Make sure that you go for one that suits not only your taste but also the personality of your dog. If possible, invest in a dog tag from a local pet store as it often engraves on site for free. You can also get the tags from a vet as well as a trusted and reputable online merchant.

Dog Leash and Lead

One fact about the dog leash and lead that you should be aware of is that the two are not the same. Both are useful but they have different functions – the leash is useful whenever you train him to walk while ensuring that he remains close to you while the lead can give him a free rein time, allowing him to explore and wander around by himself. With that said, you will also find the lead useful when letting your puppy do distance training exercises. When shopping for a lead, note that it could be as long or short as necessary. Avoid using the leash in place for a dog lead as it may only get dragged a lot through the dirt. Note that you have to maintain the cleanliness of the leash, so it is advisable to separate it as much as possible.

Once you are shopping for a leash, go for a lightweight one as it allows your Havanese to walk and wander around freely while holding it. If the puppy is around 8 to 24 weeks, then choose any leash made of nylon. While he matures and grows, though, it would be a lot better to invest in leather or retractable leash.

Dry Puppy Food for Small Breeds

You should also have a can or two of moist puppy food. You can serve this one once you notice that your Havanese eats the dry food too slowly due to his new environment and surroundings. Remember that it often takes several days to acclimate the puppy, so you need to make the adjustment as smoothly and easily for him as possible by providing him with the right food. Ensure that you also have puppy treats around for rewards and training.

Food and Water Bowl/s

It could be made from ceramic or stainless steel. Go for a dishwasher-safe one as much as possible. If your budget is tight, then you can choose stainless steel food bowls as they are cheaper compared to ceramic-based ones. In case you want to go for ceramic, then choose a high-quality glazed bowl since low-quality and unglazed ceramic bowls tend to leech lead, causing health hazards in the end.

Avoid plastic bowls. If you ever need to buy one from this material, then ensure that it has a sort of coating to prevent bacteria from penetrating and thriving. Also, remember that puppies are at risk of chewing the plastic material, so it would be a lot better for you if you look for another option.

Another tip is to choose smaller food bowls – a max of 5 inches. The reason is that there is a tendency for your puppy's ears, particularly when he grows older to land outside of his food and the bowl.

For the water bowl, ensure that you go for those that are heavy and large. Invest in a water device capable of circulating water if you are someone who needs to be away from the house for several hours once you have successfully trained the puppy.

If you go on a trip often, then you also have to invest in collapsible bowls. You can easily clip these bowls to the dog crate, making it possible to feed and water the puppy at the right time. You can then expect the bowls to go flat once unused.

Dog Treats

Of course, you also need to store some treats as such can promote further ease in training the puppy who is still new in your home. Choose high-quality treats – those that the dog will work for to get as rewards. Some examples would be benny bullies and chicken strips. Ensure that you go for treats with low sugar, filler, and wheat, too. You can also choose to offer jerky cut into small pieces as treats.

One thing to note, though, is that it is not necessary to buy the treats all the time. You can actually make some on your own. Just boil chicken breast and shred it to pieces to have some treats to offer to your dog. Other homemade treats would be cut pieces of pre-cooked ham and hot dogs. Just make sure that the treats you make are low in salt, additives, and preservatives.

Dog Toys/Chews

Make sure to also provide your puppy with toys and chews as they love to have some of these items. Among the favorites of the Havanese are usually small tunnels, climbing slides, and flat and unstuffed toys. You must prepare the toys beforehand so you can distract them from chewing or damaging cords, shoes, and furniture items around your home.

Also, remember that your Havanese puppy can still be considered a baby. With that, he will most likely take in his surroundings and identify his senses. In most cases, he will use his mouth so he can feel everything around and get to explore his environment. With the dog toys and chews around, you can give him various surfaces where he can comfortably chew on. Every time you need to redirect chewing, it would be best to have toys as they can help your puppy enjoy a wide array of surface varieties.

It is also advisable to go for tough rubber toys as those are good for teething. Some of these toys can even be filled with yogurt then freeze. You may also want to give your Havanese a couple of squeaky toys as most puppies also find such toys enjoyable. However, you should avoid spending too much on such toys as it is highly likely for your puppy to dismember them within just a couple of weeks.

Also, ensure that you go for a toy that is proven safe for your puppy. The level of safety of a particular dog depends on a few factors – among which are the size of your puppy, his preferences, and activity level. It is also crucial to take into account the specific environment the dog is in. To guide you even further, here are some tips to consider when looking for the safest dog toy for your Havanese:

- *Be wary of highly attractive and appealing toys* – Remember that in several cases, the things that dogs and puppies find attractive are also among the ones that are harmful or dangerous for them. With that said, be extra careful. Dog-proof your household by taking out the ribbon, pantyhose, kid's toys, rubber bands, and string as there is a high chance that your puppy will swallow it.

- *Pick toys that are appropriate for your dog in terms of size* – Avoid extremely small toys as much as possible since they are highly likely to get swallowed by the puppy. These items are also at risk of lodging the throat of your dog.

- *Supervise him when playing with squeaky toys* – The reason is that he may get distracted with the squeaking sound and be tempted to find it right away so he can ruin the source. This may put the dog at risk of ingesting the toy whenever he is left alone.

- *Stay away from toys without any form of dog-proofing feature* – You may also want to alter those toys without such a feature. You can do so by taking out the ribbons, eyes, strings, or any other part of the toy that you think your dog may chew off and ingest. Also, spend time checking and assessing the labels of stuffed toys.

Ensure that they contain the label "safe below three years" before buying. Examine the toys closely, too, so you can find out right away whether they contain harmful fillings. Among the fillings that may make the toys unsafe are polystyrene beads and nutshells. It is also advisable to go for soft toys that are machine-washable and discard those that begin to get torn or break into pieces right away.

Regardless of the toys you have chosen to buy, you should take responsibility for your puppy's safety by monitoring closely how he plays. If you notice him chewing pieces he should not, then take them away from him and give him another safer one.

Piddle Pad and Frame

One thing to note about the Havanese is that it is greatly possible that he already underwent training when it comes to using a piddle pad. In that case, it also helps to have this around before you bring home your pup. You can go for the plastic-backed options that feature around four layers of newspaper over it. With that, it is also possible for it to lessen the shredding. Once your Havanese matures, it is now possible for you to take out the paper. It is also crucial to have the piddle pad frame around. Go for the plastic-based one as it is already good enough to keep the pad in its place.

High-quality Comb and Brush with Pins

These items are necessary for grooming and taking good care of your Havanese. Ensure that you go for a high-quality small comb as it promotes ease in grooming your pup. Alternatively, you can choose a comb that has movable teeth, like the one offered to a cat. One advantage of having this comb around is that it seems to work ideally for cleaning the areas surrounding your eyes, though, it would be much better if the one you will be using is a parting comb if the targeted hair is longer. Remember that most Havanese have plenty of hair. With that in mind, you will notice your puppy transforming into a walking and active puffball once his hair becomes long enough.

It is also advisable to have a high-quality brush featuring pins around. Go for the shorter variation, which you should use for brushing every day, and the longer one if you have plans to use it to blow dry and lift and fluff your pup's long hair. Avoid buying a brush featuring some balls at the tines' ends, too. The reason is that it tends to cause breakage on your dog's hair. It would be better if you have both the nylon and boar bristle brush as combining them works in terms of finishing the process. Another recommendation is the mini slicker brush, which is truly effective for general grooming. You may find it useful in brushing your dog's coat or hair twice or thrice per week. Each session should last for several minutes as this can also train him a bit for grooming, preventing him from dreading it and feeling happy about it.

Nail Clippers

It is also necessary to invest in some nail clippers since you will also be responsible for trimming his nails regularly. For a start, you can take advantage of the human nail clipper. The one, which you can clip from the side, is ideal. Eventually, though, it is necessary to use the regular nail trimmer for dogs.

Toothbrush and Toothpaste

Toothbrush and toothpaste are also among the grooming supplies that you should prepare before your puppy arrives. Note that you also need to maintain the good oral and dental health of your Havanese. Choose a quality toothbrush and toothpaste meant specifically for dogs.

Bath Supplies

Of course, you also need to prepare the supplies that your puppy needs for bathing. A few of those you should invest in are the detangler, conditioner, and shampoo. Fortunately, it is not that hard to find these products as you can access many of them online and in physical stores. Just make sure to pick the most suitable bathing supplies for your Havanese. Once you already have your dog with you, a wise advice would be to wash him once every week or as necessary.

Safety Supplies

You also need to gather a few supplies that can guarantee the safety of your Havanese. One of those you should invest in is the baby gate, which you can get from any pet store or baby supply store. You may also want to invest in an x-pen, one that has puppy pads in them.

Make sure that you also have cord protectors – those that you can put over any exposed cords to prevent any electrical accidents. Another item that you may need would be a bitter apple. It has a bitter taste that will surely stop your dog from chewing, licking, or biting, a big advantage during the teething stage. Alternatively, you can buy a frozen soother or a baby oragel to make the teething process safe and convenient for your Havanese.

Chapter 9 – Preparing for the Actual Arrival of your Havanese

Now that you have completed the initial steps of acquiring your very own Havanese, including choosing a breeder, signing a contract, making a deposit on the puppy, and gathering and investing in all the things he may possibly need, the next step will be waiting for the day when you can finally bring him home. Note that once a litter gets into the hands of the breeder, they will be extremely busy making sure that the puppies will grow into healthy and happy pets.

As mentioned earlier, the Havanese breed is particularly happy, social, and loving. Each one also has a unique degree of character and personality. The breeder will be the one responsible for searching for the most appropriate home suitable for a specific puppy. It is under the breeder's responsibility, therefore, to sort out those that have show potential.

Havanese puppies who are going to be household pets will be evaluated and assigned to a home that perfectly suits their personality. This usually happens at 9 to 12 weeks. It is also the specific age when you can expect your chosen puppy to be turned over to you. You have to be fully prepared when this day comes as you can't expect everything to be the same again.

The good news is that bringing him into your household will be like welcoming a friend into your space. This means that you will most likely love the experience as the Havanese will always be a great and friendly companion. However, despite the possible good experience, you may also deal with some frustrations especially if you are unprepared.

If possible, obtain periodic updates regarding the available pup's progress from your chosen breeder while you are still waiting. Some of these updates are accurate details regarding the puppy's growth, personality, and health. The breeder also has to send you digital pictures through email or any other means as well as fun stories.

Inform the breeder regarding the call name you intend to use as this will help in making the puppy more familiar with it while it is still early. One thing to remember, though, is that while your chosen breeder is obliged to provide answers to your inquiries regarding the puppy courteously and responsibly, it is still necessary to ask and talk about what you should expect regarding updates.

Note that some breeders prefer doing it through email while others call via telephone to offer more flexibility when it comes to responding. You can also find breeders who give their future dog owners the opportunity to do a household visit after your puppy is already four weeks old. If such is what the breeder requires, then make sure that you respect the rules. Just make arrangements on how you intend to receive updates based also on the convenience of your chosen breeder.

A word of caution, though, if it is your first time owning a dog, then you may find the process tiring and exasperating. This is particularly true during the moments when you are still trying to train him what he should and should not do. Fortunately, you can minimize the frustrations at the early stages by ensuring that your home is completely prepared for him.

Planning and Preparation

When it comes to planning for the arrival of your Havanese, you should keep in mind that his first week with you is critical so make sure to focus on it. Remember that this will be the specific period wherein you can establish several things about the life of your puppy. The first week will also help him get familiar with his new environment. With that said, your preparation should greatly focus on his first few days with you.

You have to set a plan in place before his arrival considering the fact that his training starts the moment he sets his foot into your home. Ensure that you set up everything, preventing you from still figuring out what to do whenever certain situations happen. You should set a baseline when you are still starting.

For instance, you have to conduct a final examination and scrutiny on your puppy-proofing efforts before his actual arrival. Note that the Havanese is quite small, so you should avoid being complacent when it comes to scrutinizing everything that will guarantee his safety.

Do you plan to restrict your New Havanese in a small spot in your home? Then it may be necessary for you to include door gates in the items you will need to buy for his arrival. You will also need to buy some things guaranteed to help the puppy remain confined in the assigned area.

Another tip is to gather all the things that your puppy will most likely need. Ensure that the majority of items needed by the dog are around as you may no longer have enough time to go out of your house to buy such items. Before your puppy's arrival, spend time reflecting on then creating a list of the things he needs.

Spend time talking to your family, too, especially if you have kids. Remember that as a puppy new to his present environment, he will be needing the most appropriate supplies and tools to perform certain things. Your entire family should also be aware of these needs so they can familiarize themselves with what to do if you are not around.

Your preparation should also involve crafting a plan for your puppy's daily routines. Ensure that this plan is flexible since you can't expect everything to go exactly the same as you initially expected. The initial plan you set in place should just serve as your starting point to promote ease in caring for the Havanese during the first few days.

While you are training the puppy and grasped his regular and daily care routines, you should start adapting to his needs while slightly changing the routine in such a way that your puppy will only experience a sudden overturn of events. You can also tweak his schedule a bit.

However, it would be best to craft a particular schedule based on your Havanese personality and try to adhere to it just so he can easily fit not only in your family but also in your lifestyle. It is also crucial to do even more thorough preparations during the last week before your new companion's arrival. That way, he will not feel too shocked by his new environment.

How You Should Make His Ride Home Comfortable?

With the general tips mentioned earlier, you already have an idea of how you should prepare for his arrival one or two weeks before. Now, let's say that the moment of fetching him from the breeder arrives. One thing that you have to do correctly is making his ride home as comfortable as possible. It should not be frightening for him.

Note that the time you take him from the breeder so you can bring him home is also probably the first time for your puppy to ride in a car and take a long trip. With that said, certain things like unwanted and strange sights, smells, and sounds can be extremely frightening for him. You have to carefully plan for this first car ride to prevent him from getting too frightened.

Note that if you do not carefully plan for his car ride home, you will be putting himself at risk of developing issues with car rides. Ensure that this first experience will not be a traumatic one for him. In this case, you may want to apply these tips:

- *Put him in the crate* – Remember that the most secure spot for your Havanese inside the car is the crate. Your puppy may find it extremely relaxing during the ride. You will also notice that some variations on the road are soothing for your pet when you put him in his crate.

- *Ensure that you and your Havanese have a relaxed and quiet car ride experience* – In case he cries or whines, avoid punishing him. Avoid being overly affectionate, too. Doing so can only reinforce his negative behavior. If he has episodes of crying and whining, try petting him softly and wait for the situation or case to diffuse.

- *Do not forget to have breaks when the trip is quite long* – If the distance from your house and that of the breeder is kind of long, then do not forget to stop for a few minutes so you can stretch and have bathroom breaks. Stop your Havanese from going to a spot that other dogs frequent. Also, ensure that your dog is already vaccinated to prevent him from catching any disease while outdoors.

The 1st Day and Night Home

It is also crucial to prepare not only yourself but also your entire family for your puppy's first day and night home. Keep in mind that adequate preparation is necessary during this first day as your puppy may behave oddly while entering his new environment.

For instance, he will likely jump to the mix and try to fit in. He may also behave negatively because of nervousness and anxiety. You can also expect your Havanese to either sleep through the night right away or stay up the entire night while crying or barking.

Also, remember that despite being quiet and sweet, there are cases when the dog can be extremely active. This means that each Havanese displays a unique trait. He may also display various behaviors since he is still trying to figure out what is happening around him.

Once you take him home, avoid letting him roam around your house. This is important until the time when you have already housetrained or housebroken the puppy. In this case, it is crucial to use a short leash. In case you feel like he wants to rest, ensure that you are around, though, you have to remain quiet. Avoid overwhelming him with your constant excitement and affection. You should make him feel that you are around while respecting his space as he is still trying to adjust to his new environment.

It is also crucial to try making his first night in your home as comfortable as possible. One piece of advice is to ensure that you no longer give him access to food and water at six or seven in the evening. This can ensure that his bladder will remain empty. If you still give him food and drinks over that time, then it is highly likely for him to need frequent trips to the bathroom. He may want to pee or poo multiple times throughout the night. The worst-case scenario would be your Havanese ending up messing his crate.

Make sure to set aside a few minutes playing with your new Havanese puppy before putting him to sleep. Your goal here is to tire him out so he can sleep soundly. Avoid letting him nap an hour or two before his sleep schedule. This will only make him more active, playful, and energetic afterward.

During his first night, bring him outside so he can do his business before putting him inside his crate. If you were able to let him do his business outside successfully, let him know that it is a good deed by giving him plenty of praises. Doing so can help reinforce such positive traits.

It would also be helpful to observe what he needs in case he cries the first night. Find out if he wants to do his business in the bathroom or is just looking for attention. If you notice him becoming too quiet for several hours then whine or cry all of a sudden, it could be because he has to go out. Keep in mind that as a puppy, the Havanese may have tiny bladders. With that said, it would be a lot better if you set a schedule for bringing him out at least once every night.

Handling the First Few Nights

The first day and night with your Havanese is not the only challenging moment you will have to go through after taking him home. It is highly likely for the challenges to bug you the entire week, or maybe the first couple of weeks. Keep in mind that you are bringing him to a new home – away from his mother and the home he is used to.

Your Havanese may also find his new home overwhelming and intimidating even if you make him feel genuinely welcome. However, remember that you should not go overboard when it comes to reassuring him as you have to begin training the moment he steps into your home.

Avoid responding to negative behaviors right away. If you do, then it will only train him to act in such a way so he can get what he wants from you. Your goal here is to balance everything. It may be difficult and challenging to find the balance but everything is worthwhile. One of the most crucial things to train and teach him is that nighttime is not that terrifying or frightening. If you let him know that, then he can perceive your home as a place where can be safe.

You also have to set rules and let him know about them right away. For instance, if you do not want your Havanese to damage your furniture or come to it too often, then it would be best to avoid letting him sleep with you. This is important even during his early moments, days, and nights with you. Note that if you let him come close to any of your furniture, then you will be unable to teach and train him that such pieces are off-limits.

Also, keep in mind that the first few nights and weeks with your Havanese will involve a lot of noise, like whining, whimpering, and fussing. Observe such noises as those could be your puppy's way of telling you that he is lonely, scared, or uncomfortable. Keep in mind that he got used to sleeping with his siblings and mother every night, so the noises are normal and understandable. You should try stopping yourself from responding to such sounds right away.

Also, take note that the noise your Havanese makes when he is still new to your home is not the only problem you will encounter while still training him. With that, you should try to focus more on other issues, like, for instance, his comfort. One thing that you can do is to ensure that he is not too far away from you just so you will feel more comfortable. It may negatively affect your puppy since the feeling of being alone may only compound his fear in his new environment. It will frighten him more, creating the idea that he is in a scary and unhappy place.

Even if you feel uncomfortable with the noise he will probably make, ensure that he still stays with you. Avoid acknowledging the noise, too. Just let him be while letting him feel your presence. Your goal here is to reassure him, at least during the first few nights, that you will be around for him. Your mere presence would be enough to calm him down. Avoid reprimanding and punishing him during this period, too.

Also, keep in mind that part of your decision to take home a puppy will be a few nights of less sleep. It would be like a new mother welcoming her baby and taking care of her. You will lose some sleep but the good news is that Havanese puppies learn quicker compared to human babies. With that, you have an assurance that you can go back to your normal sleeping schedule quicker than when bringing him a child.

To make the first few nights even more comfortable, it is crucial to designate a sleeping area for him. It should have a crate or pen and beddings. While you need to stay in the same room with him, it is still necessary for his sleeping area to be separate from the remaining parts of your room. There should be clear boundaries that he can't escape. Ignore his whining, crying, and whimpering during this time so you can avoid reinforcing the idea that he can use such sounds to get what he wants.

Another important thing that you should do is to plan his bathroom breaks. You may set aside a small spot in his space for these breaks or take him out to do his thing every few hours. Your choice will depend on the manner through which you housetrain or housebreak your Havanese. Regardless of the housetraining method you choose, the whole scenario is to get up every few hours throughout the night so you can help him take his bathroom breaks.

The First Trip to the Vet

Another of the first few things that you have to prepare for before the scheduled arrival of your Havanese is his visits to the vet. A wise tip is to bring him to the vet during the first two days of his arrival at your home. It can contribute a lot to keeping your puppy as healthy as possible. It is also necessary for building the rapport between your Havanese and the vet.

The first couple of vet visits will be all about giving your Havanese an initial assessment. This visit will serve as the baseline that will be used by the vet in gauging the growth and development of the puppy. The first few visits to the vet with you as the new owner of the puppy will also usually involve a new puppy examination or wellness check. It is also the time when your puppy's vaccinations will be scheduled.

Do not forget to bring the shot records and health certificate of your puppy to the vet as the information here will immediately let the vet know more about the health of your Havanese. The health records will also give the vet an idea regarding the vaccines already received by your pet.

One thing to note regarding the first few vet visits is that such will also leave an impression on him. It is possible for him to want to explore the whole office as well as socialize with the other pets in there. In other words, you can also use this time to begin socializing him, though, you also have to be extra careful when doing so.

Ensure that you ask permission from the other pet owners before allowing your Havanese to socialize with them. This is to prevent his first encounter with other pets from turning into a horrifying experience. Also, ensure that the other pets and animals he gets close to are not in pain, sick, old, or excessively wary or uninterested in a puppy with a lot of energy.

Allow your Havanese to approach only those pets with mellow personalities and are genuinely interested in socializing with him. That way, your puppy will also have a positive encounter. You can always get the idea about whether it is okay to approach the other pet or if your Havanese is unwelcome by getting the permission of the pet owner or the one accompanying the other.

Another thing you should take note of is that older or aging animals may not like the idea of getting approached by another pet. Some of them can't keep up with the energetic Havanese. In such a case, you should respect them by not letting your pet come near them and cause them discomfort.

Aside from that, you have to give your Havanese positive feedback whenever he displays positive or good behaviors in the vet clinic or office. Be affectionate and comforting, too, as such will let him know that the clinic is not synonymous with fear and torture. By rewarding your Havanese and letting him stay in a positive environment, you have an assurance that he will remain at ease even when doing vet visits.

Chapter 10 – Dog-proofing Your Home

Dog-proofing your home should also be one of the first few things you have to do for your Havanese. Keep in mind that this breed is highly energetic, which means that you have to dog-proof your home and turn it into a truly safe place for your new buddy. When it comes to pet-proofing your living space, it is safe to say that you can't expect anything to be safe as far as what a pet can access.

To guarantee the safety of your Havanese, it is advisable to have a holistic perspective of your household environment. It is also crucial to figure out the specific parts of your home requiring some pet-proofing. It is a basic and essential aspect to prepare for once your pet's scheduled arrival comes close. With effective dog-proofing, you will feel at ease. You can finally let your guard down without worrying too much about the safety of your puppy and dog.

Kitchen

For the majority of pet owners and parents, the kitchen is where they usually prepare and make the meals and the specific spot where the pet asks or begs for food. An important reminder, though, is that food and hazard can be perceived similarly considering the fact that a lot of delicious foods that are safe for humans, like onions, coffee and chocolate, are actually toxic to pets.

With that in mind, you have to know exactly what foods are toxic and unsafe for your Havanese and ensure that he can't reach them easily. Store foods properly and ensure that your garbage can in the kitchen has a secure cover. All cleaning products also need to be out of your pet's reach.

Bathroom

Another part of your home where your Havanese can get in and out to is the bathroom, so you need to make sure that this place is completely safe for him. Note that if he gets into your bathroom, then it is highly likely that he will do a lot of unwanted stuff, like shredding toilet paper and drinking the water in your toilet. Luckily, several of the possible damages he may do while inside your bathroom are minor.

However, there are still instances when he can put himself in serious trouble especially if he gets in touch with harmful household items, like cleaners, medicines, and other products commonly seen in the bathroom, such as potpourri and drain cleaner. Find out what could harm your dog while inside the bathroom, so you can take them out beforehand. Also, make sure to store away all potential hazards. They should be out of your Havanese's reach

Living Room

The living room is usually the spot where your Havanese will frequent as this is also where you and the entire family gather together to relax and bond. The many things inside your living room, like furniture items and appliances, can turn the place into an unsafe spot for your Havanese if you do not dog-proof it. You need to pet-proof some items in this cozy place, like your furniture and carpet, as your pet can quickly and easily damage them.

You also need to tuck away electric cords. Your pet should not be able to access them easily. If you have a fireplace in your living room, then make sure that you also invest in a protective screen installed in its front part. If you have plants as part of your home décor, then remember that there are also common plants cultivated inside the household that can be toxic and poisonous to your pet, so be extra careful.

Bedroom

If you will allow your Havanese to get inside and stay in your room, then you also have to do something to make it safe for him. Note that similar to the other rooms within a household, the bedroom also has a few potential hazards to pets. Among them are exposed electrical cords, medicines left on your bedside stand, and curtain cords. Ensure that anything that may put your Havanese in danger or poison him is stored out of his reach and vision.

Outdoor Area

Aside from the rooms inside your home, you also have to make sure that your outdoor area is safe and secure for your puppy to roam around. The most important tip when it comes to pet-proofing the outdoors, though, is to do something to prevent your dog from getting outside willingly.

As a pet parent, you need to exercise more caution around the windows and doorways. Ensure that your dog can't easily jump or dash for it. Another thing you should avoid is your pet falling accidentally. If possible, you should have your Havanese microchipped, so you can easily find him just in case he disappears or escapes from your home.

While it is kind of challenging to prevent your Havanese from getting out of your house on his own, you can still guarantee his safety by ensuring that the outdoors is properly pet-proofed. There should not be too many safety hazards for him. Aside from that, he also needs to roam around under your proper supervision.

Some of the potential hazards you should prevent your dog from accessing are:

- Pesticides and chemicals for the lawn

- Compost piles

- Fertilizers and mulches

- Ponds and swimming pools

- Poisonous plants

- Insects, including ticks and fleas

Ensure that the yard also has a proper fence. With that, you have an assurance that your puppy will not be exposed to a lot of threats out there. Note that the outdoors has several potential hazards and risks but you can prevent them from causing damage to your Havanese by having a well-maintained and solid fence for your yard.

Additional Pet-proofing Tips

Now that you are aware of the specific areas that may expose your Havanese to plenty of safety hazards, it is time to learn more about the basic tips and tricks that you can implement to guarantee the effective and successful pet-proofing of all parts of your home. Among these tips are:

- *Gather all the needed pet-proofing supplies* – The ones you often use to childproof your home are also the ones that can help keep your dog out of danger and trouble. Fortunately, most of these supplies are inexpensive plus easy to install. Try to visit a local baby store and shop for the following items that are proven useful in pet-proofing your home:

    - Baby gates – Use them in limiting the access of your pet in the rooms in your home that are frequently used.

    - Safety locks for bathroom and kitchen cabinets

    - Power strip covers

    - Electric outlet covers

    - Containment system, which you can use in organizing all your electric cords

Have all these items ready and you will surely be able to provide your Havanese with a safe environment – one that he will enjoy staying in for quite a long time.

- *Ensure that your trash cans are securely covered* – Note that your garbage cans are home to smells that your curious puppy may find exciting and interesting. With that said, you need to securely cover them.

  Without the cover, your puppy will be at risk of consuming something in your garbage that is toxic for him, such as xylitol gum. It is also highly likely that he will swallow an object, which can trigger internal obstruction. Another potential risk is his head getting trapped in a snack bag, which may suffocate him. By putting a cover in the garbage can, you can make your puppy avoid all those risks.

- *Have proper protective cover for your cords* – Make sure that you also have protective covers for any exposed cords in your home. A sturdy cord cover or a deterrent spray placed on your chargers, power cables, and electric cords can be a big help in protecting your puppy from possible burns affecting the mouth as well as from accidental shocks.

  Yes, you need to supervise your Havanese puppy all the time, especially if he is not in his pen or crate, but you also have to make sure that everything he touches or gets exposed to will not put him in danger.

- *Stow bags properly* – Ensure that all your bags, including your backpack, purse, diaper bag, and gym bags, are properly organized as there are instances when some of the items inside them can be threatening and dangerous to your new Havanese. One of these is xylitol, which is present in products like hand creams and sugar-free gums.

  It is harmful to the Havanese as it can lead to poisoning. Unintentional or accidental poisoning is a common pet emergency, so it is advisable to store and organize your bags in a closet with doors. Alternatively, you can organize them in a durable hook installed high, making it impossible for your Havanese to reach them. With that, you can prevent your puppy from being exposed to anything inside your bag that may harm him.

- *Set aside a drug-free zone in your home* – It should be a place in your home that does not have any form of medication. Keep in mind that human medication is a common cause of poisoning in pets yearly, so ensure that you store all your supplements and medications in secure drawers and cabinets.

Do not just leave them to sit on countertops or nightstands that your dog can conveniently and quickly reach. Aside from that, you have to put the medications your pet is using separate from yours. If there are spills, dispense the liquids and pills over the bowl or sink, too. That way, you can prevent your pet from ingesting them that may lead to harming them.

- *Identify the specific houseplants that are poisonous to the Havanese* – Note that while houseplants may look innocent, they are also at risk of causing mild to severe problems to your puppy – among which are mild irritation, organ failure, and digestive upset. There is also a risk of death, especially if your puppy nibbles on the plants.

  Among the harmful plants that may poison dogs and other pets are Sago palm, castor bean, autumn crocus, and American yew. Prevent your dog from being exposed to these poisonous flowers and plants to guarantee their safety.

- *Keep potential poisons away* – Apart from the poisonous flowers and plants, there are also other products and supplies in your home that might poison your Havanese. With that said, you have to puppy-proof your home in such a way that all these supplies are not within his easy access.

Some of these products are glue, detergents, household cleaners, and automotive and yard chemicals. Lock up all these toxic substances to prevent your dog from even coming close to them and accidentally ingesting them.

- A lot of pets also find antifreeze enticing, so be extra careful whenever you need to clean spills and store containers. Other items you have to keep out of reach of your Havanese as they are often toxic to him are slug baits as well as mouse and rat poisons.

- *Do not forget to set a boundary in your home* – There should be limits. Considering the fact that the Havanese breed is naturally curious, you can expect him to try exploring several parts of your home with the goal of testing their limits.

One way to set up boundaries is to install baby gates that your dog can easily see and follow. Also, close any appropriate door to prevent your dog from reaching places that you think are unsafe for him.

- *Ensure that your Havanese remains grounded* – Remember that as a puppy, your Havanese will most likely have fragile bones. It is also highly likely for his clumsiness to come out since he is still young. With that said, you should do something to prevent your Havanese from getting injured in case he tries to jump and fall down accidentally.

  One thing you can do is to have a seat on your couch to prevent the possibility of an injury. Another tip is to prevent your puppy from getting into tall furniture. You have to take extreme caution in this area until you notice your puppy building up his strength, thereby making him more coordinated and less fragile.

- *Prevent your Havanese from easily accessing battery-operated items* – These include electronic toys, remote controls, key fobs, or anything that requires the use of a battery. Do not let them just scatter on the floor. Keep them at the right places, specifically out of your puppy's reach.

  The reason is that apart from the fact that it may cause him to chew and swallow minor

117

parts, it may also lead to him swallowing the battery, which is even more harmful. If that happens, the soft tissue within the esophagus of your pet may be at risk of getting burned, so be extra cautious if you have these items at home.

- *Eliminate the clutter* – Before you ever take your Havanese home, make sure that you have already eliminated all the clutter and mess from your home. Remember that puppies love to chew even your valued items, including your designer glasses and branded shoes.

- You can prevent potential damages to your items by keeping them in their proper places, preferably out of his reach. The scheduled arrival of your Havanese should also serve as your signal that it is indeed time to declutter and reorganize your home.

Dog-proofing your home may seem like a daunting and time-consuming task, but the results are all worth it, especially once you feel at peace knowing that your Havanese will be safe under your care. It can eliminate those incidents when your puppy eats your sofa or raids your garbage since it lets you restore order in your home through pet-friendly solutions.

Chapter 11 – The Havanese Diet: Learning What You Should Feed Your Havanese

Now, let's move on to one of the most important aspects of caring for your Havanese – his diet. You have to know exactly what you should feed your puppy as such will ensure that you will be giving him the right foods all the time, particularly those that meet his nutritional requirements and needs based on his age, activity level, and lifestyle.

Your Havanese will only be able to bring out his incredible personality if you give him all the nutrients that his small and adorable body needs. This chapter will cover some of the suggested foods that can perfectly meet the requirements of all Havanese regardless of their actual size and shape.

You will also get an idea about how much you should feed this breed to prevent them from overeating. Basically, almost all things that you have to know about the Havanese diet form part of this chapter.

How Much Food Does Your Havanese Need?

Before starting to buy dog foods that are perfect for the Havanese, it is crucial to learn more about nutrition so you can provide him with what his body needs exactly. One important point you should remember, in this case, is the fact that he is pretty little. Since this breed only weighs around 7 to 14 lbs., the food he needs to eat is a bit lower compared to larger dog breeds.

However, you should constantly remind yourself about the importance of finding the perfect balance between too little and too much. It is the key to ensuring that your dog will receive enough food and nutrition. In most cases, a typical 10-lb. Havanese puppy who has a normal activity level requires around 342 kcal daily.

However, if the Havanese is more energetic and active, then you may need to provide him with more foods – up to 545 kcal daily. This should be enough to keep up with his higher activity level. Once he gets older, you can also expect his active personality to dwindle a bit.

He will become a bit less active, which can prompt you to lessen his kibble to around 280 kcal daily. Also, remember that these dogs are small, which means that you do not have to feed them too much. It is even crucial to regulate and control their meals to prevent them from overeating.

Essential Nutrients Needed by the Havanese

Your Havanese needs certain nutrients for him to thrive and grow into a healthy and happy dog. With that said, you have to make sure that the foods you feed him offer a good supply of the following nutrients:

Protein

Just like when protein is vital for every human being, it is also crucial for the health of your Havanese. A higher amount of protein is even needed especially for more active consumers. It plays a crucial role in developing muscle mass. One thing to note about the protein or amino acid is that it can either be plant-based or animal-based.

If you have a Havanese, the animal-based one is a better option. Aside from being healthier for them compared to the plant-based ones, animal-based protein is also easier to digest for them. With that said, pick dog foods mainly based on meat, such as turkey, whole chicken, fish, mutton, beef, duck, bison, or venison.

Most Havanese dogs crave such food items the most. If you intend to buy commercial dog foods with the mentioned varieties of meat, then make sure to read the labels carefully. Find the major and main ingredients. Go for those marked to have animal-based protein specifically.

Healthy Fats

Your Havanese also needs a good supply of healthy fats. Despite being classified as healthy fats, they are not around to trigger weight gain on your Havanese. They are even critical for the overall health of your puppy, provided you only supply them in moderate amounts. The good thing about letting your pup ingest sufficient amounts of healthy fats is that they can support their active and energetic personality.

The essential fats in their foods can supply them with sufficient energy that will help them have all the energy they need for the whole day. Apart from being supportive of their energy and active lifestyle, healthy fats are also crucial in maintaining the good health and shine of the long and silky coat of your Havanese.

As much as possible, supply your puppy with animal-based fats, such as fish oil. The reason is that they are the healthiest versions of fat for dogs that can also promote better heart health. Moreover, these fats are easier for the liver and metabolism of your dog. Just make sure to keep each portion small and retain sufficient calorie consumption so your pet can get the most out of these fats.

Do not forget to check the label of the food products, too. Ensure that the label states for animal sources, such as fats taken from chicken fat or salmon oil. They are among those that the body of your dog can easily absorb. You may also want to use plant oils as they can balance Omega-3 and Omega-6 – both of which are essential fats you can often find in various dog food products and recipes.

Carbohydrates

Carbohydrate is also a key nutrient in a Havanese diet. One reason is that your Havanese needs carbs in order to sustain the energy required by his lively personality. Keep in mind, though, that the key is moderation. You should still avoid feeding him too much as excessive amounts of carbs may hamper his health. In low to moderate amounts, these carbs will be vital to his overall health as such nutrients contribute to the elevation of his energy.

Complex carbs should compose a minimum of 25% of the food consumed by your Havanese. Some sources of these complex carbs are whole grains, legumes, beans, and veggies. These are the carbs that can supply your dog with the energy or speed he needs to perform playful and active activities and finish his chores. Also, ensure that you get carbs from digestible sources while preventing the protein content from getting too high. It should only be a max of 5%.

Fiber

Your beloved Havanese also needs a good supply of fiber. It is highly recommended for around 5% of his daily diet to contain fiber. This nutrient is essential for the life of your Havanese as it can maintain the strength, good health, and efficiency of his gut. Apart from creating the necessary bulk in your puppy's intestines and stomach, fiber is also essential in smoothing out the pooping process.

Other Essential Vitamins and Minerals

Your Havanese also needs some of the vitamins and minerals present in other foods, particularly in fruits and veggies. You can even find a lot of companies that primarily manufacture foods adding supplements to their products to increase their power and nutrition content.

When shopping for food for your Havanese, some of the vitamins you should look for are Vitamin A, Vitamin C, Vitamin D, and Vitamin E. Such vitamins are crucial for the health of your puppy as they can protect him from various diseases, like those linked to his muscles, eyes, and bones.

What the Havanese Diet Should Not Contain?

While certain nutrients should be present in the daily diet of your Havanese, there are also those that should be avoided. Ensure that the foods you feed your Havanese do not contain any of the following as they may put them in danger:

- **Raw Foods** – The majority of raw foods, especially raw meat, are not good for the health of your puppy. With that said, ensure that his diet does not contain such raw ingredients or products. Aside from causing an upset stomach, these raw foods may also hamper the oral and dental health of your puppy.

- **Excess Sugar** – Just like humans, sugar is also one of those food ingredients and items that can cause harm to your puppy. With that in mind, you should avoid giving your Havanese too much of it. You can give him fruits recognized for containing sugar but ensure that you do so in moderation. That way, you can prevent your puppy from consuming too much sugar that is bad for his overall health.

- **Artificial Preservatives** – You also have to be extra careful when preparing the diet of your Havanese so you can prevent them from ingesting harmful artificial preservatives, like BHA and BHT. These artificial preservatives are notorious for being toxic to pets, particularly dogs. With that in mind, you have to ensure that the food products you are buying do not contain them.

- **Additives** – Check the additives integrated into the dog food products you intend to buy or use for your homemade dog food recipes. Some additives you should avoid using are taste enhancers, colorings, preservatives, and flavorings as they can trigger the development of major ailments, such as cancer.

By ensuring that what you feed your Havanese does not contain any of these harmful and toxic ingredients, you have an assurance that his health and body will continue to be in tip-top shape.

Basics of Feeding the Havanese

One fact about the Havanese that matters a lot when it comes to feeding him is his people-centric attitude. His people-centric nature is one reason why you can expect him to be devoted to you so it is highly likely that he will always look for you for his basic feeding needs. Also, be aware that most Havanese dogs are insistent. With that attitude, there is a great possibility that he will nibble, nip, and beg for food throughout the day.

Fortunately, this breed is also capable of sending signals in terms of the ideal feeding schedule. However, the curious nature of the Havanese will also cause him to just take one or two bites, come back to you to grab your attention, then go back to his food. It would be like he is asking for a feeding buddy. If this scenario happens, then remember that it is normal. Do not reprimand him for it or discourage him from doing so, unless this behavior gets overboard that it tends to become annoying.

As far as the feeding schedule is concerned, your Havanese puppy will most likely need feeding around three to four times daily. The rule of thumb would be giving him around one-fourth cup of his food during mealtimes. Also, do not forget to take away his food bowl after around fifteen to twenty minutes as this will serve as his encouragement to eat faster.

You should also follow these guidelines based on what stage of life he is in:

- **Puppy** – Just like what has been mentioned a while ago, a Havanese puppy needs to eat at least 3 to 4 times daily. His small size prevents him from consuming the required amount of food in just one to two meals so you should try to divide it into 3 to 4 smaller meals.

  Also, make sure that your Havanese puppy receives around 8% crude fat and a minimum of 22% crude protein daily. This is essential for his healthy growth and development. You should also remember that the active and alert personality of your Havanese also means that his metabolism works fast.

  Taking that into account, you should offer nutritious foods that are not heavy on his tiny stomach. One way to handle this is to go for a dog food brand, which manufactures products specifically for the toy or small breeds.

- **Adult** – Your Havanese puppy can be considered as an adult upon reaching twelve months. When he reaches this age, you can transition him to a form of diet specifically made for adult toy dog breeds. One thing you may notice in the labels of adult dog foods that are compatible with the needs of the Havanese is the consistently high protein ratio.

  However, you will also notice a reduction in the calorie content as it aims to prevent the dog from becoming overweight or obese. You do not have to worry about this lower calorie content. Remember that the dog food is already good for your dog provided it contains added supplements, such as chondroitin and glucosamine that can strengthen joints and improve his immunity.

- **Senior** – Your Havanese will probably hit his senior stage upon 7 to 8 years old. It is the time when he begins to slow down. Once he reaches this stage, you have to pay closer attention to his daily diet. You need to make sure that you provide him with foods that can help him even as he gets a bit slower.

  Also, note that reaching the senior stage means that his once healthy metabolism will begin to falter. The health of his teeth, joints, and bones will be affected, too. In that case, remember that you do not have to lessen his food consumption that much. You should set a goal of making his diet as nutritious as possible.

  Find a food formula, which takes into account the specific requirements of a senior toy dog breed. With such a food formula, you can expect your Havanese to receive all the nutrients he needs without worrying about him gaining excessive pounds.

One more thing you should remember is that once your Havanese becomes a senior, two or three meals daily is enough. Do not forget to check the instructions on the food package so you will get a clear idea of how much you should feed your dog based on his age. Avoid unnecessarily increasing the recommended dose as it may only lead to excess weight or obesity.

Is it Safe to Feed a Havanese Human Food?

When it comes to creating the proper diet plan for your Havanese, one question that may have crossed your mind is whether or not it is safe to feed this breed with human food. The answer is it depends on what you feed him. Yes, the Havanese breed can eat human food but you have to make sure that you pick the most sensible food choices – those that are not toxic and harmful for your dog specifically.

Also, remember that just like you, your Havanese also needs to consume a balanced diet, so you should be extra careful and wise in selecting the human foods that you intend to feed him. It is the key to optimizing his health regardless of age. This is also the principle followed by most dog food companies. All of them are already aware of the right balance of nutrients, fats, minerals, proteins, as well as other ingredients and elements capable of improving the health of dogs.

With that, buying from them may be the most sensible choice for you. However, this does not mean you cannot feed your dog with whatever you and your family are eating. It would be best to wait for your Havanese to become an adult before feeding him human food, though. You should avoid feeding your Havanese puppy human food as he is still in the developing stage.

His digestive system is not also ready to take in the foods of humans considering the fact that it is still in the stage of development. Feed him the foods recommended for him during this early stage so you can help in boosting his growth until he reaches adulthood.

Once your Havanese grows into an adult, you can finally let him enjoy the foods you are eating. Just make sure that you are already completely aware of what foods are safe and non-toxic for him. Some safe food choices for your adult Havanese are:

- **Boiled chicken** – It is probably the easiest food you can prepare for your dog. You can also expect him to love it. Choose the boneless skin-on thigh when boiling as it has the perfect balance of delicious taste and good nutrients. However, if your dog has issues with excess weight, then you should consider boiling skinless and boneless chicken breast for him as it is healthier.

- **Hard-boiled egg** – Another great idea would be a hard-boiled egg, which is a great way to make your Havanese get protein. Give him just half of the egg, though, since the protein here is not as easily digestible as that derived from meat.

- **Steamed or boiled vegetable** – You can also offer your adult Havanese a serving or two of steamed or boiled vegetables. What is great about this food option is that it lets him receive sufficient fiber. The majority of boiled

130

vegetables actually work great for the Havanese breed but you should still make sure that the veggies you are feeding him do not have even the slightest sign of harm to him.

Among the safest vegetables you can feed your Havanese are red tomatoes, green beans, carrots, and pumpkin. Avoid cabbage, cauliflower, and broccoli as they tend to cause some potential issues in the health of the Havanese. Make sure that you do not feed garlic, green tomato, and onion to him as those are proven harmful for dogs.

- **Homemade biscuits** – It is also very rewarding to prepare homemade biscuits for your dog. Fortunately, it is not that hard to make them nowadays as you can find several recipes online. When preparing biscuits, though, make sure that you lower the butter and sugar content. This is to prevent your dog from gaining too much weight, which may result in health problems later on.

- **Apple** – Apple is also healthy for dogs. You can offer half of one apple to your dog so he can receive its benefits. Just make sure that you take off the core of the apple as well as its seeds as those may be toxic to your dog plus they are kind of hard to digest. Once you have removed the harmful parts of the apple, you will have peace of mind feeding him with it as it can supply him with plenty of nutrients that are good for his health, including Vitamin C, fiber, and potassium.

- **Banana** – This fruit is also safe for your Havanese to eat. You can give one-half of a piece of banana if you notice your dog hungrier than usual. It could be because he spent too much of his energy on exercise or when playing. Just a bit of it can already make him feel full plus it has fiber.

If you want to give your Havanese the chance to try other types of food apart from the usual commercial dog foods, then you can let him taste the ones that humans eat. Just make sure to research those foods that are 100 percent safe and non-toxic for your dog, so you will never put him at risk.

Chapter 12 – How to Train Your Havanese?

The Havanese breed is famous for its intelligence, so you can rest assured that you can also easily train your puppy. However, the adorable nature of the Havanese may also sidetrack and distract you, which means that if you are not careful, you will end up causing his bad behaviors to overpower the good ones.

With that in mind, it is necessary for you, as the dog owner, to be consistent during the training. It is also advisable to stand firm whenever you teach him something. It is the key to transforming him into a loving and well-behaved member of your family.

Crate Training

Crate training should form part of the entire process of raising a well-behaved Havanese. The first thing you should do is to put the crate in a spot where he will not feel completely isolated, such as the family room, living room, or kitchen. Avoid putting it in a somewhat isolated place, like in your garage, a closed bathroom, or basement. Doing so may only cause your puppy to feel like he is abandoned, making it harder for him to adjust to his new environment.

Ensure that the crate you have invested in for him is big enough that he will not have a difficult time turning around and laying down. Avoid going for an extremely large one, though, as it may only cause him to potty on one part of it then utilize the other parts for sleeping. It is also advisable to put a towel or old blanket – one that you can easily launder – for his bedding. However, avoid putting the bedding if he tends to potty on the crate.

Once your Havanese puppy starts relying more on the crate, you can make it larger. You can give him a chewie or safe toy whenever you put him in a crate but ensure that you avoid giving him over one toy. If you have purchased several toys for him, then rotate them to continue gaining his interest.

Whenever you command him to go inside the kennel or stay in his crate, do so using a happy voice. Give him a treat and praise when he follows such command, too. That way, you can instill in his mind that the crate is safe for him.

Crate training will also become easier with the following tips:

- **Encourage your puppy to get inside his crate** – Note that your Havanese puppy might hesitate to get inside the crate the first time he sees it. It is the reason why you should put something to encourage him to get inside. You may want to put small pieces of delicious treats near, inside, and at the back of his crate.

  Be patient even if it takes several minutes, even days, for you to encourage him to enter the crate successfully. Avoid forcing him, though. Let him get inside at his own pace. You can somehow increase his motivation to enter this area through verbal praises, so he can associate the crate with only positive things.

Once he gets used to his crate, you can leave its door open, allowing him to enter and come out of it anytime he wants. If he is already comfortable entering his crate, you can begin training him to eat his meals inside.

- **Close the door of the crate during mealtimes** – If it is still your first time to close the crate's door, make it a point to reopen it prior to him even finishing his meal. Increase the amount of time spent on leaving the door closed with every meal gradually.

You can increase the length of time for several minutes until you are already capable of keeping it closed for up to 15 minutes after every meal. Make sure to only open the door when he no longer whines. The reason is that whining could indicate that you are rushing to increase the length of time you can close the door after the meal.

In that case, open the door only after he has finished whining. If you notice that he whines constantly, then you may want to consider shortening the amount of time you spend keeping the door closed after he can eat his next meal then increase it gradually.

- **Keep the door of the crate closed for up to several hours** – If your Havanese continues to look calm after you left the room for half an hour, then he may also feel comfortable handling longer periods of being enclosed in his crate. It would be better for you to practice putting the Havanese inside the crate for several hours. You can also do so overnight.

One more thing you should remember is that the Havanese has a risk of developing separation anxiety. With that in mind, his crate training should start if you want to let him stay in the crate for a prolonged period. Another tip is to give him toys, like food puzzles, so he will be busy while waiting for the time he can get out. Just don't forget to let him or ask someone to take him out to eliminate.

Another point to remember is that the Havanese puppy is incapable of holding his bladder for long stretches. With that said, you should take him out to eliminate after letting him stay inside for several hours. Overnight crating also requires bringing him out to pee or poo during the night. Watch out for cues that he has to eliminate, too, like pawing the door of the crate and whining.

- **Make him perceive the crate as a place where he can sleep** – You can do that by picking him up then putting him inside the crate whenever you notice that he is already sleepy or actually sleeping. Once you transfer him to the crate, allow him to settle down then fall asleep once again. Also, spend a couple of minutes sitting by the crate so you can pet your

Havanese until the time when he settles and sleeps.

- **Learn how to manage his whining** – Every time you hear your puppy whine while inside the crate, you may have a hard time ignoring it. This is especially true if you are unsure if his whining is due to him wanting your attention or needing to eliminate. If your Havanese is still too young, then it is highly likely that the whining inside his crate means that he would like to eliminate.

  In that case, take him out to eliminate immediately but bring him back to his crate right after. Do so without interacting or communicating with him. If the reason for his whining is his need for attention, then note that he may quiet down if he realizes that such an act will not grab your attention.

Crate training should focus more on forming positive associations. Do not commit the mistake of other Havanese owners who ended up forcing or pressuring their puppies to get inside the crate without establishing that it is a safe, secure, and positive place for him first.

Your goal should be to encourage your Havanese puppy to believe that nothing bad will happen to him inside the crate and that goal is achievable by creating and facilitating good associations.

Potty Training

The entire Havanese training process should also involve serious potty training. One thing to note about this breed is that they tend to poop or pee after napping, eating, drinking, sleeping, playing, or whenever they get excited. Use the fact that he needs to go several times throughout the day to your advantage. Remember that each lesson counts as it can ingrain good habits in him.

During the first two days or so, take your Havanese out on a leash approximately every hour. It would be best to do this after he eats and sleeps. Bring him to the specific spot where you designate for his potty. You can then command him with any word you want that he can easily associate with the need to pee or poop (ex. go potty).

After those first two days, you can slowly increase the gap of taking him outside. However, you should still be consistent in teaching him and showing him the exact place where he should eliminate. If he does it successfully, give him rewards. The entire potty-training process requires patience since you can't expect him to get what he needs to do right away, but just keep repeating it as frequently as possible, and he will surely associate the place you designated outside for his potty soon enough.

Also, remember that it is kind of time-consuming, taking up to 6 to 8 months. It is roughly the length of time when his bowels and bladder stop developing. With that, he will have more control over himself.

This period can also provide enough time for him to grasp mentally what he is supposed to do whenever you bring him to the toilet.

To have an easier time potty training your Havanese during this period, you can use these tips:

- **Use a leash** – A leash can prevent your dog from wandering too much while you are still training him to increase his comfort level on the floor. Invest in two lengths – one that is around four feet in length while the other should be at least five feet. The shorter leash is helpful in keeping the dog close to you while the long one has to be used outside every time you bring him to potty.

  Avoid tying the leash to anything. Also, ensure that you stay with your dog without any form of distraction whenever you are using the leash on him. Avoid letting the leash go as it may only cause your Havanese to wander around. You may want to tie the end of the leash around your waist so your hands will still be free to do other stuff while he is with you.

- **Take advantage of a cage** – Another thing that you can do is to place your Havanese in a crate or cage. Do it in such a way that he will feel comfortable during the early stages of his life. It is also a big advantage during his early training and development. Put a puppy pad inside the cage where he can do his business.

However, use it only during those nights when he is sleeping in the bed. Keep the puppy pad at the cage's opposite end. It should be far from his dog bed. When it comes to potty training your Havanese this way, one thing you should remember is to avoid leaving him inside for prolonged periods as it may only make him feel lonely and isolated.

- **Invest in a litter box** – A litter box is a great option for potty training your Havanese if you are someone who lives in a high-rise building or a busy city wherein taking him outside to potty is challenging. In this case, gather similar supplies like the ones used for a large cat breed. After setting it up, ensure that you maintain its cleanliness as it will encourage your puppy to use it.

- **Let him use a bell** – Potty training will also be easier once you successfully train your puppy to use a bell. Install this bell close to your backyard's doorway as much as possible. Your puppy should also be able to reach it with ease. It will let you train him to paw at the installed bell as a way to alert you every time he wishes to go potty.

- **Observe for signs** – Get to know more about your Havanese from the moment he steps on your home. Keep a close eye on him so you will know the signs he may use to communicate that he needs to go. If you notice such signs, take him to the intended spot. Avoid carrying him to the spot, though. It would be best to walk him there, so he will get used to walking to the intended pooping area on his own eventually.

- **Stick to a consistent schedule** – As much as possible, let him go potty on a consistent schedule. It promotes ease in ingraining the habit in him. You can use it to remind him about the specific time and place where he should eliminate. With that, it will be quicker for him to form such a positive habit. Remember that with the intelligence of the Havanese, he will be able to catch the behavioral patterns soon enough.

Probably, the last and the most important tip that you can implement when it comes to potty training your Havanese is to give him positive reinforcements. You can do so by rewarding and praising him for every successful business at the designated spot.

The most effective positive reinforcements for him would be the things he loves and craves, like additional lap time and his favorite treats. Let him know that there will be nice treats waiting for him for successfully eliminating at the intended spot. This will be a source of encouragement to do better during the training process.

Socialization Training

The Havanese is a naturally social animal – one who seems to love being with everyone. However, you still have to encourage him to bring out this natural personality through proper training. Note that if you do not properly introduce him to other pets and people during the puppyhood stage, he will be at risk of developing a timid attitude, making him suspicious of everyone around him, especially strangers, and look distant and standoffish.

With that said, it is a necessity to provide your dog with various experiences that will socialize him properly, such as meeting visitors at home, as well as children, other dogs and pets, and strangers in a public setting. The most important tip would be to start slowly socializing him the moment you take him home. Early socialization conducted properly and continuously all throughout his lifetime can help him grow into a well-adjusted dog capable of handling all situations that come his way calmly.

Focus on giving him continual and thorough socialization at the earliest possible time. Doing so can prevent him from being wary and territorial of strangers. Expose him early to various animals, places, people, and situations. The socialization training should also focus on taming his behavioral patterns, which is usually all about trying to eliminate all unwanted behaviors, like aggressiveness, anxiety, fear, and excessive barking.

Socialization is not actually that hard to do as it just involves exposing him to a lot of things – be it people, kids, other dogs, pets, and animals, and various places. It can give you peace of mind knowing that you get to expose your puppy to a wide range of situations while gaining an assurance that he will seek guidance whenever he is looking for rules of etiquette whether outdoors and indoors. It will serve as your dog's foundation throughout his lifetime.

In that case, begin such a form of training during his first three months. Dedicate this period to exposing him to as many new animals, people, environments, and stimuli as much as possible. However, do it in a way that you also avoid overstimulation as it may lead to withdrawal, avoidance behavior, and excessive fear. To avoid that, proper socialization should begin prior to the complete vaccination of your puppy.

Some vets also highly recommend maximizing every safe opportunity of exposing puppies to various stimuli during this time. One example would be to enroll him in puppy classes. The good thing about this tip is that it can improve his training, strengthen his bond with humans, and let him socialize in a specific environment where there is a low risk of illness.

These classes are also capable of providing your puppy with an organized and safe approach towards socialization. It contributes to boosting his ability to respond to commands.

Direct all your efforts to expose him to everything, too. As much as possible, encourage him to investigate, explore, and manipulate his environment.

You can enrich his environment through various surfaces, tunnels, chutes, steps, interactive games and toys, as well as other forms of stimuli. If possible, let him accompany you on many of your car trips. Continue these forms of exposure until he becomes an adult as it is the key to maintaining his sociable and outgoing personality.

As for training him at home and giving him socialization classes at the comforts of his new environment, positive reinforcements are necessary. It is possible by giving him praises and rewards frequently. You can also reward him with additional playtime and petting.

However, during the socialization, it is also crucial to schedule some time for your Havanese puppy to play on his own. During this time, he can enjoy his favorite toy. You may also want to let him spend his alone time taking a nap in a safe place, like his puppy pen or crate. It is helpful in teaching him to amuse himself, thereby preventing problems linked to overattachment to you.

Another important precaution during the socialization process is to prevent visiting parks or other places without proper sanitation. Avoid exposing him to places known to have a high traffic of dogs without vaccination, too. This can prevent your dog from contracting unwanted diseases and infections during the course of his socialization training.

Obedience and Command Training

Basic commands serve as the foundation of your puppy's overall obedience training. By letting your puppy master even simple exercises, such as stay, come here, paw, down, and sit, you can be closer towards your goal of raising an obedient and intelligent Havanese in all possible areas.

Apart from command training, you may also want to teach him some tricks. Luckily, there are several benefits to giving him this form of training. For one, it allows the both of you to bond. The fact that your puppy is young and receptive also means that he can quickly pick up the commands and tricks you are teaching him.

It also paves the way for easier training if you want him to learn more advanced tricks and commands once he grows up. For the command training to work, try following this basic outline:

- Give your puppy just one new command.

- In case he is still unfamiliar with the given command (ex. it is still his first time hearing it), try giving him physical aid so he will be able to grasp its meaning.

- Repeat the command and observe whether or not he already gets its meaning.

- Give him a reward in case he successfully assumes the commanded position – The reward could come in the form of his favorite

145

treat. You may also want to shower him with praises.

- Continue saying the command – Repeat it as many times as possible until he automatically assumes the position whenever you say the command word.

Aside from that basic command training structure, you should also try to implement these do's and don'ts during each training session:

- Make the training as simple for him as possible – Your goal here is to set him up to win and succeed. Also, remember that he will only respond to positive reinforcements, so make sure to prepare the necessary rewards.

- Conduct the training without any distractions – That way, you can let him focus on following your commands.

- Perform the training after he receives his daily dose of exercise – Make sure that he has eaten prior to the training, too.

- Avoid showing your frustration in case he makes mistakes – Remember that he will be able to sense such a negative emotion, so avoid showing it as much as possible.

- Stick to a single command or word – Avoid changing it frequently as unnecessary changes may only confuse your Havanese.

- Practice consistency – Be consistent in giving him his command training every day.

- Increase the difficulty – The training should also involve increasing the level of difficulty whenever your Havanese masters one command. For instance, you can make it more difficult by introducing some distractions.

In addition to the mentioned tips, it also helps to continue his basic command training daily even after he has already mastered a few command words. This can contribute a lot to training your Havanese to become a more obedient pet.

Chapter 13 - Behavioral Training

It is also essential to prioritize the behavioral training of your Havanese. Note that your goal for training is to raise a well-behaved dog, so you have to correct any unwanted and bad behavior that your Havanese puppy is displaying right from the get-go. Just like all other forms of training, you should begin with the ones linked to establishing good behaviors the moment he steps foot in your home.

In that case, start by showing him that you hold the alpha position in the house. This means you are his master, instead of the other way around. It would be best to start training him the basics at around 6 to 8 weeks. Show him that you have full control over his schedule, mealtimes, toys, as well as the things he loves and enjoys. That way, he will start respecting you and looking at you as the alpha of the household.

Also, keep in mind that all members of the family are over your dog. This means that you also have to teach them the need to show your Havanese that there are rules that he needs to follow in the house. Apart from creating a schedule on feeding, exercise, potty times, playtimes, and others, ensure that you also focus on correcting the following behaviors:

Chewing

A Havanese pup has the tendency to chew things for a wide range of reasons – one of which is boredom that usually happens if you do not stimulate him enough through exercise or play. It could also be because he is teething. In that case, he may chew on things to deal with the pain and discomfort associated with it.

Other possible emotions that may cause him to display chewing behaviors are anxiety, nervousness, and fear. This is a bad habit that you have to correct and fix as soon as possible. The best thing that you can do is to target the problem immediately and get rid of the temptation as much as possible.

You may also fix his chewing habit through the following:

- **Give him chew toys** – The goal for giving him chew toys is to let him know the right places to direct his chewing. This can teach him not to chew on other stuff, like electrical wires, clothes, and shoelaces, among many others. If he chews the toys, praise and reward him. He needs to receive repetitive praises whenever he uses the right chew toys.

- **Set limits on his area every time you are not around** – Designate a spot for him whenever you are away. Make sure that this spot does not have a lot of bad chew temptations. The place also needs to have his toys. It aids in reinforcing the idea that it is okay to chew but on the right items and toys.

- **Give him enough physical and mental stimulation every day** – Provide him with enough exercise. Let him go through training sessions every day, too. Be consistent when doing so. By letting your dog know what to expect every day, you can encourage him to display good behaviors and ditch the unwanted ones, including inappropriate chewing.

Excessive Barking

The Havanese makes an incredibly alert dog considering the fact that this breed does not bark that much without any reason. If he barks, then you can easily curb it by blocking his view so he can stop whatever it is that is causing him to display such a behavior.

The problem comes when he seems to bark excessively, which is unnatural for this breed. In that case, it could be because of human error. Fortunately, this specific behavior is something that you can fix with the aid of simple tips, including the following:

- **Ignore his excessive barking** – You may think that this tip is counterintuitive but take note that most dogs, including the Havanese, actually function based on kid logic, which means that they consider all kinds of attention a good one. In other words, acknowledging his barking may only cause you to give him the attention he is seeking, thereby further encouraging and stimulating such behavior.

With that said, start ignoring his excessive barking tendencies. Wait for him to quiet down on his own. If he does, praise him in the form of a treat. It is also possible for you to integrate a command to this, like "quiet". Say such a command whenever he stops barking then give him the intended praise and reward. This can contribute a lot to making him associate such a command with him stopping down his barking.

- **Get rid of all temptations that encourage barking** – In case he barks excessively whenever he sees people passing by from your window, the best thing that you can do is to block his view from it. You can block off all access to the source of his barking to avoid such a situation completely.

- **Give him enough exercise** – Make sure to exercise his mind, too. The goal here is to try to lose all his excess energy through physical and mental exercise. If he has already spent all his excess energy, then he will most likely behave well.

True, the Havanese does not require excessive amounts of mental stimulation and exercise, but you still need to give him brain exercises and some playtime. The goal here is to prevent him from getting bored, which will only increase the possibility of him seeking other sources of entertainment – some of which may result in excessive barking.

- **Provide alternatives to barking** – Your Havanese should have other things to do rather than bark unnecessarily. By providing him with alternative activities, he will be preoccupied physically and mentally. For instance, give him his favorite chew toy before someone you invite over to your house arrives.

Apart from the mentioned tips, it is also crucial for you to stop the urge to yell at your dog with the goal of quieting him down and controlling his barking. Never reprimand him harshly as doing so may only worsen this behavior in him.

Be consistent in training him through other means, though – for instance, through positive reinforcement. You may also want to assess how severe his barking is. For extremely severe cases, a complete lifestyle change may be necessary for the two of you.

Fear and Anxiety

The fact that the Havanese is a gentle breed also makes him prone to displaying fear and anxiety, especially if he is exposed to a negative situation or if he is underexposed. Also, remember that you can expect this breed to respond better to positive reinforcement compared to punishments, like hitting or yelling.

Aside from requiring a gentle hand, you also have to be extra mindful of how you act and behave if you know that your Havanese is somewhat fearful and anxious. Remember that if you display negative behaviors towards him, then it is highly likely that it will exacerbate his fear and anxiety.

It is also crucial to talk to your veterinarian and ask for help in searching for a professional behaviorist if you notice that the fear and anxiety of your puppy are becoming too severe to the point that it significantly affects his quality of life and mental well-being.

You may also want to implement desensitization and counter-conditioning to manage your dog's fear response successfully. Desensitization refers to a process wherein you slowly expose your puppy to the stimulus that triggers it. On the other hand, counter-conditioning involves training him to display a trait or behavior, which is different from his present response to a trigger or stimulus.

Also, remember that just like all forms of training, the most effective way of building a positive association is to provide plenty of rewards. Make sure to look for specific rewards valued by your Havanese puppy. It could be in the form of a toy or food. You just have to make sure that he loves it. It should grab his attention regardless of how overwhelming a certain situation is.

To desensitize your Havanese, here are some tips you can apply:

- *Expose your puppy to the stimulus he is afraid of at a distance* – Do this slowly. For instance, if he loves hotdog but fears strangers who wear hats, then you can seek the help of a friend and ask him to wear a hat while standing at a distance. He needs to be close enough that your puppy can acknowledge that he is around.

   However, your friend also needs to be far enough, so your Havanese can still take bites of his favorite hotdog comfortably. In case your puppy displays signs of fear or does not acknowledge your presence nor take a bite of the hotdog, then move the trigger further away from him. Do this until he can finally relax.

- *Slowly reduce the distance between the trigger and your puppy* – Do this until he is close enough to your friend. When that happens, you can ask your friend to toss some treats for the Havanese to enjoy.

This technique is extremely helpful when trying to make your puppy associate the thing that he is afraid of with the thing he loves. It allows you to replace his fear response with the feeling of anticipating something good.

One thing to remember about desensitization, though, is that it is a long process, so it is advisable to take things slowly. Also, remember that while some dogs are capable of showing significant improvements within just a short period (within a day or two, for instance), others need more time to let go of their fears.

In this case, you have to stay patient and consistent. Be positive all throughout the process, too, and soon enough, you can eliminate the unnecessary fear and anxiety of your Havanese.

Chapter 14 – Dealing with Separation Anxiety and Other Destructive Behaviors

Another possible issue with the Havanese that you may have to correct at the earliest possible time is his vulnerability to separation anxiety. Note that as a dog breed guaranteed to be people-driven and affectionate, your Havanese puppy will most likely want to spend most of his time with you and other people. He simply will not love the idea of being alone. With that in mind, he is vulnerable to dealing with separation anxiety.

Whenever he gets separated from you or from anyone he grows attached to, he will most likely bark excessively and unnecessarily. He may also be at risk of injuring and biting himself. With that in mind, it is crucial to determine some basic tips in handling this problem, so you can prevent him from displaying unwanted behaviors associated with a high level of separation anxiety.

The first thing you have to do is to determine the signs that your Havanese indeed has separation anxiety. That way, you can adhere to a technique that works specifically for him.

Some signs indicating that your puppy has this chronic canine disorder are:

- Clinginess

- Tendency to destroy objects

- Excessive barking or yelping

- Persistent screaming and howling

- Hyperactivity

- Urinating or defecating in inappropriate places

- Diarrhea

- Vomiting

- Too much salivation

- Trembling and pacing without apparent reason

- Depression every time he thinks or feels like he is alone or will be left alone soon

Most of these symptoms of separation anxiety will become more visible whenever you decide to leave him on his own at home. It may also happen even before you actually left your house. As soon as he notices some signs that you are leaving the house, his separation anxiety symptoms may start appearing. Apart from learning about the symptoms, it is also crucial to find out the specific causes of the condition. It could be that you fail to remind your Havanese that as the owner, you are also the one who is supposed to be his master or leader. This means that you should be the one controlling the situation, instead of him controlling you. It also means you should stop attending to him right away whenever he cries on his crate. Another example is to avoid picking him up whenever he displays unwanted behaviors, like slapping and howling. You do not have to punish him in those cases but you should ignore such behaviors, especially if you know that there is no valid reason for them. Note that during those instances when you do not properly ignore his bad and unwanted behavior, you are also cultivating the mindset that those were rewarding and acceptable.

Avoid giving in to his negative behavior, especially during training as it may cause you to be unable to ingrain in his mind that you are his master. With that, it could trigger separation anxiety since he will grow more attached to you. You have to show him who is in charge and in control of the house. Insufficient exercise may also cause your Havanese to develop separation anxiety. Note that if he has excessive amounts of energy stored up, then he will probably start showing off behavioral issues, including separation anxiety. Leaving him alone will even magnify his stress level, leading him to act out even more since he does not have an outlet for using all of his excess energy. Give him enough exercise by walking him around the neighborhood or even just around the yard. You are allowed to do it anytime at night and in the morning. Another potential cause of your Havanese developing separation anxiety is a sudden and significant change in the schedule he is used to. For instance, you may have taken a few days off from your work so you can stay with your puppy, at least during the first two weeks. The problem is when your leave is over and you have to go back to work. Think about how he may feel if you suddenly leave him alone for several hours every day after he has been used to spending the entire day with you. Such significant and sudden change may cause him to develop separation anxiety, which you can avoid by starting to train him right after he gets inside your home.

Managing Separation Anxiety

So what can you do if your Havanese starts displaying signs of separation anxiety, especially if those are severe? Here are a few things that can soothe them in such a case:

- **Give him exercise** – The goal here is to tire him out before you leave him home. Some dog trainers even recommend bringing your dog out for a long walk or jog before leaving him alone. If he is tired enough, then he will no longer have any energy to do something destructive because you left him for a while.

- **Leave calmly** – Make sure that your departure from your home is calm. This is to prevent stressing out your Havanese even more. You may want to say something soothing to your dog or give him a treat for not making a fuss before you leave.

- **Put on some background noise** – Another effective tip whenever you need to leave a Havanese dog who seems to have separation anxiety is to play some background noise. The sound could come from the television or the radio. The goal here is to muffle or conceal any sound that may trigger his anxious behavior every time you leave the house.

- **Condition him to absences** – You can do that by leaving him for a few minutes then coming back. You should then gradually increase the length of time you leave him until he gets used to the fact that there are indeed instances when you will be absent from his sight.

- **Prepare a safe place for him** – It could be a puppy pen or crate – just as long as it can help him feel safe and secure. Make it fun and exciting for him by adding some of his favorite toys so he will not feel so anxious once he notices that you are not around.

- **Let him have some alone time** – This tip is something that you should do even if you are at home. For a Havanese with separation anxiety, this tip also works by letting him stay with you in a room but without letting him sit on your lap.

For instance, he is in his pen in a room where you are also staying. This means that he can see you, though you have to make sure that he is not right beside you. You can then train him to be alone eventually by working your way up towards letting him stay in another room without you.

- **Add structure and routines to his daily life** – The goal in implementing this tip is to let your dog be aware of what to expect during his day and when it will happen. It can make his day more predictable, promoting ease in leaving him alone every now and then and reducing his stress level.

  One thing that you can do to make his day as structured as possible is to have a set schedule for feeding, training, playing, and taking outdoor walks. You also need to set rules, though, you also need to make sure that they are easy ones, so you can easily enforce them consistently.

  Some examples of these rules would be requiring him to sit and wait every time you open the door of his crate and doing something prior to giving him a treat. Again, be consistent as knowing what to expect is also a big help in building his confidence.

- **Use essential oils** – Many dog owners also say that using aromatherapy and essential oils can help relax your dog, especially during stressful moments (ex. when he is fully aware that you are about to leave). Use a diffuser and a few drops of essential oils. The scent produced here can make your stressed Havanese feel relaxed, making it easier for you to leave the house without worrying about him reacting negatively.

- **Invest in a dog camera** – A dog camera is a fantastic investment as it gives you the chance to monitor your dog whenever you are out of the house. With this device, you can always check in on how your canine is doing. Apart from that, it allows you to hear him and speak to him. There are even dog cameras that let you throw your pet a treat.

  However, keep in mind that you can't still get a hundred percent guarantee that letting your Havanese hear your voice is effective in soothing him. There are even instances wherein it can worsen his anxiety. Still, there is no harm in trying this valuable device that already helped a lot of dog owners in dealing with their pet's separation anxiety.

When it comes to managing the separation anxiety tendencies of your Havanese, you should remember how important it is to build his resilience. You can do that by boosting his independence and confidence. While it is truly fulfilling emotionally to have a dog who wants to be with you all the time, remember that it could still turn into a problem later on. Your goal for trying to manage his separation anxiety is to make him more independent and resilient, which is also helpful in your attempt to build a happy and fulfilling life together.

Dealing with Destructive Behaviors

Your Havanese is undoubtedly an adorable pet but as you can see in this chapter, this breed is not exempted from showing destructive behaviors. Yes, chewing, digging, and being territorial are normal behaviors for dogs but these same behaviors also become problematic and no longer normal if they turn into destructive tendencies. This happens when such behaviors lead to your dog destroying things, like shoes, carpets, doors, and furniture.

If your dog digs in an incorrect place or chews on inappropriate things without any other accompanying symptoms, then his condition can be categorized as primary destructive behavior. If he displays other symptoms, including fear, aggression, and anxiety, apart from the destructive behavior, then his case is secondary destructive behavior. Remember that if left untreated or unmanaged, such behaviors can also result in problems with his other organs, including his teeth, intestines, stomach, and skin.

How to Diagnose Destructive Behaviors?

Considering the fact that certain destructive behaviors affect a lot of Havanese puppies, there are times when it is necessary to have this problem professionally diagnosed by a vet. In this case, you need to visit your veterinarian and inform him that you suspect that your Havanese has separation anxiety issues.

During the diagnosis, your vet may request a complete behavior and medical history of the puppy. This information is crucial in establishing patterns and in ruling out or confirming physical conditions that also have a possible link to your pet's behaviors. Among the information you have to prepare as they may be asked by the vet are:

- Training history of your puppy

- Level of physical activity every day

- The specific time when he started showing destructive behaviors

- How long has he displayed such behaviors?

- Usual events that seem to trigger his destructive behaviors

- Is he alone when he displayed destructive behaviors?

Also, inform your vet whether your dog's destructive behaviors got better, remained consistent, or worsened from the first time those were displayed.

The vet will also perform a physical exam to find out if the dog has signs of a medical condition that triggers the behavior. Among the examinations that will be conducted are complete blood count, urinalysis, and biochemical profile. The results here will give your vet an idea regarding the presence of any problem in your puppy's internal organs.

The vet may also conduct a test to determine the level of his blood thyroid hormone. This will let him know whether he has an extremely high or low thyroid level. Note that there are also instances when thyroid hormone imbalance can lead to destructive behaviors. Other tests that your vet may conduct would be stool and blood tests as well as magnetic resonance image (MRI) and computed tomography (CT) scan.

All these tests and exams are necessary for scrutinizing every part of his body, including the brain, and assess overall functionality. Those are essential in figuring out whether there is a tumor or brain disease, which triggers the display of behavioral issues. If the vet did not detect any medical problem, then expect your Havanese to be diagnosed with a behavioral condition, specifically separation anxiety.

Treating Destructive Behaviors

If after all the tests the vet did not detect any medical condition in your puppy, a plan will be developed, which aims to treat the behavioral problem. The treatment plan often involves a mix of medication and training since you can't expect to resolve the issue with only medication.

If the social anxiety of your Havanese triggers him to display primary destructive behaviors, like chewing on house plants, furniture edges and legs and small objects left in your house, as well as excessive digging of holes in your yard, then the vet may create a treatment plan designed to direct your puppy's destructive behaviors and acts towards appropriate objects.

With that, you can train your dog to chew on appropriate things and prevent him from damaging things in the house if he inappropriately chews on them. The good thing about primary destructive behaviors is that they no longer require medication. An effective prevention plan and training will be the only thing that your vet will recommend to you.

As for secondary destructive behaviors, both training and medications are necessary for successful treatment. You will know that his condition falls here if he tends to destroy things with the sole purpose of grabbing your attention. With that, expect to be around when he displays destructive behaviors as his goal will be to let you see him do those things.

If that is the case, your vet will most likely prescribe an anti-anxiety medication as a means of helping your puppy respond quicker to the entire training. Both you and your vet may also have to establish a training plan, which teaches your dog to behave more appropriately.

The moment he understands that it is bad to destroy and damage objects, you can finally stop his anti-anxiety medication. However, remember that he may also need to be treated using the anti-anxiety medication for quite some time so he can recover from his destructive behavior.

Managing the Destructive Behaviors During the Treatment Process

Once you begin the training and medication for your Havanese, expect your vet to communicate with you often to monitor the effects of the program on you, the dog, and other people in the house. Ensure that you follow what is prescribed by the vet to the letter. This means giving medications in the exact way it was directed by the vet.

If there is a prescribed medication, then expect follow-ups from the vet, too, together with complete biochemistry profiles and blood counts. These follow-up checkups and tests are essential in finding out whether the medications have adverse effects on the internal organs of your pet. Ensure that you do not let your dog take other unprescribed medications.

Also, remember that your patience will be put to the test during the treatment period. With that said, be more patient during the entire process of teaching your dog to eliminate his destructive behaviors. Remember that it may turn into a slow process. It can even take at least a few months to complete. There are even instances when your Havanese will be more reluctant and anxious to learn new behaviors. In that case, his training and medication will be longer until he feels confident on his own.

Just be a patient dog owner if that happens as you and your pet will surely be rewarded once the treatment plan is successfully completed. Eventually, you will be rewarded with a well-behaved dog who knows exactly how to behave appropriately in various situations and environments.

Chapter 15 – How to Take Care of His Health?

In general, the Havanese breed is recognized for being healthy with a life expectancy spanning from 12 to 15 years. There are even Havanese dogs who exceed such life expectancy because they are generally healthy. Most of the dogs under this breed are also capable of going through life without major health problems.

It could be because of the diligent health testing done by reputable breeders, particularly those who seriously and responsibly take their role as guardians and stewards of the breed. Most of them walk the extra mile to guarantee the excellent health of their dogs and even go through the point of testing them against heritable health conditions.

However, even with the guaranteed excellent health of the Havanese, you can't expect them to have zero risk of acquiring health problems in the future. You need to know that there is still a limited possibility for your puppy to develop health issues, so you have to do thorough research and ask your chosen breeder questions.

Basically, among the health conditions that seem to affect the generally healthy Havanese are the following:

Cataracts

A cataract refers to a condition characterized by opacity or diminished transparency in the eye's lens. In several cases, you can see the opacity being confined to a tiny part of the lens. There are also cases where it affects the entire structure. A severe case of cataracts, which may affect both eyes, can lead to blindness. If the cataract is just small and minor, then you can rest assured that it will not affect the vision of your Havanese.

A cataract in dogs is actually the same as the one experienced by humans. It happens when a thin film starts forming over the eye's lens, which can obstruct one's vision – whether it is a dog or a human.

The majority of cataract cases in puppies and dogs are actually of the genetic type. Take note, though, that the Havanese is more prone to developing this eye condition compared to other purebred breeds. It is the reason why it should be part of your priorities to have the eyes of your Havanese checked for this condition every year.

Cherry Eye

Another condition affecting the eyes and vision that the Havanese is prone to developing is the cherry eye. It often happens when the gland's base flips up. You can see it behind and above the third eyelid's border.

One thing to note about the third eyelid is that it is a structure shaped like a triangle that you can find in the internal corners of the actual eyes of your dog. It sometimes covers the dog's eye partly. You can also see it consisting of t-shaped cartilage capable of providing not only a tear gland but also adequate support. The third eyelid is extremely necessary for your eye surface's protection as well as in the production of tears. If the gland is prolapsed, then expect it to become inflamed and appear swollen. Though you can expect the swelling to recede after just a short period, it is highly likely that it will remain prolapsed. Note that it is an extremely important and major tear gland. With that, you need to preserve it as much as possible. The cherry eye condition often affects young dogs, so your Havanese puppy is prone to it. There is also no confirmation yet if it is an inherited or genetic condition but it seems like some breeds are predisposed.

When this happens to your Havanese, remember that surgery may be necessary as a means of anchoring the cartilage and gland back into the correct position. Also, remember that the prolapse can recur occasionally. Never remove the gland as it may cause the insufficient production of tears that may lead to other conditions.

Chondrodysplasia Punctata (CD)

CD refers to a medical disorder affecting the Havanese, which causes his leg to grow unevenly. It may also be characterized by bowed legs, dwarfism, and disparity in gait, which results in lameness. This disorder, therefore, affects skeletal development and may significantly affect the growth and development of your Havanese.

There is also what is referred to as osteo chondrodysplasia, which encompasses a group of disorders, including the closing of growth plates prematurely characterized by the cartilage and bone growing abnormally. Such disorders often lead to skeletal dwarfism characterized by your puppy's formed limbs being crooked or bowed and disproportionately short.

To diagnose this condition, a visual gait exam, physical exam, and a couple of X-rays may be conducted. There are also instances when corrective surgery becomes a requirement but note that this does not happen all the time.

If your Havanese seems to possess a crooked front, then it is necessary for your vet to examine him physically so there will be an accurate diagnosis. The X-rays, on the other hand, will be necessary for confirming the accuracy of the diagnosis and determining if other abnormalities requiring treatment are apparent.

Consulting your vet is also necessary if your puppy shows signs of lameness, like difficulty in walking or standing up, reduced activity level, and a bunny-hopping gait. Another thing to remember is that bones often stop growing once your puppy reaches around a year old. If a surgical procedure is needed for CD, then there would be a higher recovery rate if performed during the development stage of your puppy's bones.

Hip Dysplasia

Another of the most common health conditions that may affect your Havanese is hip dysplasia. It usually takes place whenever the socket and ball of your dog's hip joint improperly form. If this happens, it can likely trigger tremendous pain, which is only curable through surgery.

Basically, the condition can be described as any abnormality in the way your dog's hip joint develops. For instance, if a loose fit is noticeable in the bones here as well as the ligaments designed to help in holding them together, then it is highly likely for the ball to slide partway from the socket.

One fact about hip dysplasia that you should know is that it tends to occur showing only a few or zero clinical signs. A clinical sign exhibited by your Havanese regarding this problem is probably lameness in one or two rear limbs. It is also possible for a severe case of arthritis to develop due to hip joint malformation. It can lead to pain, especially as the ailment progresses.

Your vet may start suspecting that your Havanese is suffering from hip dysplasia if there are noticeable lameness and pain in his hips. To make an accurate diagnosis, though, your vet may conduct an X-ray to assess how the pelvis and femur fit. In most cases, it is a requirement to do the X-rays while your dog is under anesthesia or sedation.

This is crucial in ensuring his proper positioning when the X-rays are taken. If your dog has been detected to have hip dysplasia, then be aware that the only means of treatment would be surgical and medication.

Patellar Luxation

Patellar luxation is a common condition in the Havanese breed characterized by the loose formation of the elbow joint. It usually occurs when the patella or kneecap pops out of the dog's luxates or joints. It may affect one or multiple elbow joints. This condition may also trigger a chronic case of temporary lameness.

Patellar luxation is also categorized into various grades and categories with the signs and symptoms of the condition varying depending on the luxation's degree. However, it is usually linked to lameness in any of the hind legs. If this affects your Havanese, then take note that this condition can be corrected through surgery, though, this treatment approach is not a necessity.

Liver Shunt

The liver plays a crucial role in the body in the sense that it works in clearing toxins – most of which can be described as protein digestion by-products derived from blood. Liver shunt happens in dogs when a part of blood sidesteps the liver, causing it to reach the heart directly. This is actually a bad thing as it causes toxins, particularly ammonia, to accumulate in the bloodstream while leading to signs of neurological issues.

Some symptoms you may encounter would be poor appetite, seizures, lethargy, and weakness or disorientation. Note, though, that kidney disorders may happen in your dog if he has a liver shunt. If you want to control this condition for your pet, then stick to a special diet. It may be necessary to undergo a surgical procedure depending on the exact location of the shunt.

A lot of canines that have congenital liver shunts tend to display clinical symptoms prior to reaching six months. If your dog only shows subtle signs, then the accurate diagnosis may only happen at a much later age. Also, remember that the signs of a liver shunt are quite vague but they often include depression, poor balance seizures, blindness, disorientation, weakness, and sudden loss of appetite.

Deafness

Your Havanese is also prone to developing hearing issues – one of which is deafness. One way to determine if a canine is deaf is to let him go through the hearing test called (BAER) or brainstorm auditory evoked response. This test aims to check whether your canine is suffering from deafness. Both ears also have to be tested individually. Overall, the test will be complete in just ten to fifteen minutes.

To lower your chance of owning a deaf dog, you should contact responsible breeders and deal only with those who have successfully completed the testing and vaccination of puppies. Note that a sign that you are dealing with a responsible breeder is when you will receive the results of the BAER test prior to replacing it. It is also crucial for both parents to be tested.

Havanese dogs who are unilaterally or bilaterally deaf have to be neutered or spared. It is crucial to avoid breeding even during those instances when only one parent is deaf. As a new dog owner, make sure to ask the breeder regarding BAER testing. It is also advisable to consider if the puppy and parents are confirmed to be truly healthy.

Legg-Calve-Perthes (LCP)

This is another potential disease that may affect small dog breeds, like the Havanese. It impacts the hip joints. It basically takes place when the hip's ball part of your Havanese gets damaged because of an inadequate supply of blood. You can expect the symptoms to be noticeable at around five to twelve months. Such symptoms include pain and limping. There are also cases when it can lead to arthritis.

To confirm if your pet has LCP, a couple of X-rays may be conducted. As for the treatment, it will vary depending on how severe the signs of the condition are. It is possible for the muscles in the leg affected by the disease to experience atrophy. If this specific atrophy symptom is severe, then there is a chance that it can significantly slow down the period of recovery. In that case, you can't expect medical therapy to work as you initially expected.

The best course of treatment in such a case is surgical. The process will involve removing the femur's head and allowing the muscles to develop a false joint. Most of the dogs who underwent this procedure were able to recuperate well, which is safe to say that it is an effective treatment. While the exact reasons for developing LCB are still unclear up to this moment, there is an assumption that this problem has a genetic component.

Suggested Pre-tests or Examinations for the Havanese

Just like what has been indicated earlier, while your Havanese is generally healthy, it still does not mean it will not carry diseases in the future. It is the reason why you have to seriously think about closely working with a reputable Havanese breeder who focuses a lot on the health and wellbeing of their dogs.

Go for a breeder who goes the extra mile to pre-test breeding pairs to ensure that their breeding lines retain excellent health profiles and records. Dealing with such a reputable breeder can also save you from preventable heartaches regarding the health of your Havanese in the future.

Prior to committing to a breeder, request a copy of documentation that shows the required health exams and tests at present. If you are dealing with a reliable breeder, then expect him to share this information without any problem. At present, the health tests recommended by the Havanese Club of America to every intact, non-neutered and non-spayed, prospective breeding puppies and pairs are the following:

- **BAER test** – It means brainstem auditory evoked response. With the BAER test, it is possible to detect single-ear (unilateral) or both ear (bilateral) deafness. This non-invasive test, which only takes around 15 minutes, aims to detect any hearing impairment in the Havanese as early as possible.

- **CERF/CAER test** – This essential health exam aims to figure out whether your Havanese is suffering from cataracts or dealing with an eye issue that is specific to the breed. It is an annual test as each exam is good for only a year. It is a non-invasive test, though, it requires eye dilation.

- **Patellar evaluation** – Another test that the Havanese, or any dog breed, for that matter, has to go through is the patellar or knee evaluation. What this test does is check for patellar luxation, which refers to a condition characterized by a loose knee joint. This condition may occur in at least one joint. The entire test makes use of radiograph (X-ray) technology as a means of examining the joints in the knee closely, but expect it to be completely non-invasive.

- **Hip evaluation** – The main goal of this test is to detect hip dysplasia in a dog. It is a condition characterized by a malformed ball and socket joint found in at least one hip. This test will closely examine your dog's hip joints with the aid of radiograph (X-ray) technology. It is non-invasive, making it safe for dogs.

Ensure that your chosen Havanese goes through all the mentioned tests to guarantee that they do not hold any major health issues that can greatly affect their life or general wellbeing. One thing to note, though, is that most purebred dog breeds at present have an equal chance of inheriting specific health issues.

It could be because of the focused breeding that needs to adhere to a purebred standard. This fact should not deter you from buying a dog, though. It should just serve as an invitation to screen breeders carefully so you will be one hundred percent sure that what you are getting is healthy.

Also, it would be best for you to ask if the breeder offers an initial health guarantee that lasts for around 12 to 24 months. If the breeder does, then make it a point to grab it. Ensure that you also let your new puppy get examined by your chosen canine vet within a day or two after picking him up.

It will let you detect if it has any signs of illness from the start. Also, remember that most of the diseases affecting the Havanese are hereditary. Fortunately, they are not high-risk conditions. Some are environmental diseases that you can easily avoid by providing your dog with proper attention and care.

Chapter 16 – Basics of Grooming Your Havanese

The spirited personality and abundant silky hair of the Havanese are probably among the major reasons why many find this breed an adorable companion dog. However, just like other dog breeds, it is also important to dedicate some time when it comes to grooming him. The Havanese also takes pride in its non-shedding coat, which is one reason why it perfectly fits those who are prone to allergies. However, you need to groom him regularly in order to maintain the excellent condition of his coat.

Routine Bathing and Grooming

This breed requires bathing and grooming on a routine basis. With his abundant double coat, you may need to bathe him as often as one week or every three weeks. The decision on how often you will bathe your Havanese will depend on not only the amount of his coat but also his lifestyle.

One thing to note when it comes to taking care of the Havanese is that caring for and maintaining his coat can set a strong foundation for keeping both his coat and skin healthy. Bathing him regularly can promote the proper growth of his coat, too. It can prevent the excessive buildup of dirt that may cause it to tangle and mat.

However, take note that each time you bathe your dog, there is also a possibility for him to lose the natural moisture and oil in his coat that makes it look glowing and smooth. This fact should influence the number of times you should bathe your puppy. The key is proper balance based on the lifestyle of your dog as well as his environment.

For instance, if your living space is in a place with a constantly humid and warm climate, then bathe your Havanese only once every month or only during those times when he is extremely dirty. If it is in a place with a colder climate, then you can lessen the number of times you bathe him. If he is not too dirty, then sprinkling him with some baby powder would be enough to maintain the cleanliness of his coat.

You need to keep his coat as clean as possible as the buildup of dirt may cause the hair shaft to break down because of roughness. This can lead to further damage. Once it is time to bathe him, make sure to follow these steps and tips:

- **Wet his coat then put on the shampoo** – The best way to apply the shampoo is to squeeze it through his coat using a downward motion. You can guarantee the thorough cleaning of your dog's coat by moving the shampoo down his coat. You need to shampoo his coat thoroughly as it is the key to strengthening it and making it as healthy and manageable as possible.

- **Condition the coat** – Follow a similar application as when you are shampooing his coat once it is time to apply the conditioner. Conditioning his coat should form part of his bathing routine as it is crucial in nourishing and hydrating each hair strand.

- **Rinse the coat** – After putting on the conditioner, you can rinse your puppy's coat. It would be best to let the water temperature cool down a bit and use it during the final rinse. This is a big help in completely removing all the products used in his coat.

- **Use a towel to blot the coat** – Do this once you have completed his bath. Make sure to squeeze all excess water from his long furnishings, legs, and ears. It is advisable to implement downward movements when removing the excess, instead of circular motion, as it can help in preventing tangles.

  Alternatively, you can use a blow dryer after bathing. Just make sure to use the lowest setting while gently brushing out his hairs. Start from those layers that are closest to his skin. Choose a wide-tooth metal-based comb or brush when handling the body. As for his face, it would be much better to use a smaller comb made of metal.

Does your Havanese have a long coat? Then it would be better to use a stand dryer. You may also do line drying. What you have to do is to line dry his whole coat systematically. Do it down to his skin. Ensure that your puppy is fully dry in the specific spot you are currently targeting before moving on to another section.

After ensuring that he is fully dry, the next thing you have to check is whether or not he is already tangle-free. You can do that by spending a couple of times brushing his coat with the metal comb. You will know that his coat is already free of tangles when you can let the comb glide freely through it down to his skin.

Working with Tangles

If the hair of your Havanese has mats or tangles, then it is advisable to detangle first prior to giving him his regular bath. In this case, you may want to use a detangler solution, which you can buy in any store providing pet products. Alternatively, you can use a combination of dog conditioner and water.

Just apply this mixture or the ready-made detangler to his coat then pull a wide-tooth comb gently through his tangles. Be extra careful to avoid pulling out your dog's hair. Also, be extra careful to avoid cutting out knots. The goal here is to untangle his matted hair gently using a mat-and-tangle comb or your own fingers.

Another thing that you can do to manage your puppy's mats and tangles is to comb his coat regularly. Examine the coat regularly for tangles to prevent the formation of severely tangled or matted fur. Coat grooming is also necessary for your Havanese every day.

How to Clean Up the Face?

Most Havanese boast of hairy faces. While this looks adorable, the hair on the face is also prone to get littered with dried dog foods as well as other things that their muzzles may get in, such as soil, grass, gravel, and leaves. To keep his face clean, focus on cleaning up his mouth, nose, and eye area first. You should then get the liquid tangle remover spray and use it in smoothening tangles from your dog's facial hair.

Once applied, let the detangling solution stay in his matted or soiled hair while combing or brushing his body. The time when you have already finished combing the limbs and torso may also be the time when the solution is already absorbed in your dog's facial hair.

In that case, it may have started working its magic, especially when it comes to loosening the tangles. After working on the tangles, you can get the fine-toothed comb and use it in combing the remaining parts of his face.

Hair Trimming

When it comes to clipping or trimming the hair of your Havanese, it would be best for you to seek the help of a professional. However, if you already own the tools needed for trimming and clipping, then it is possible to provide your Havanese with the trim he needs at the comforts of your own home.

Do the trimming after you detangled, bathed, dried, and combed his hair. Once you have completed that, you can begin trimming with the help of dog clippers. Start at the sides of your dog's face then swipe the clippers from over his ears then down to his cheeks and beard. After that, you can use a pair of thinning shears for trimming the hair found at both his eyes' inner corners.

The next step is getting a comb then trimming the hair found at both sides of his muzzle. Comb the topmost part of his head then round it off. Afterward, begin trimming the hair found beneath the ears, as well as on the jawline and cheeks. The next thing you should do is combing the hair found on the ears then trimming them in such a way that it will result in a rounded shape. Trim the exterior corners of both his eyes just in case you prefer highlighting his eyes.

When it comes to trimming, remember to avoid doing it on excessive amounts of hair. The reason is that if you trim or remove too much hair, then your Havanese may no longer be able to showcase his natural physical attribute, which is his adorable hair and coat.

Avoid shaving down the coat to his skin, too. The reason is that it may only cause your puppy to be more prone to sunburn as well as other prospective ailments that may lead to skin cancer and infections.

Eyes

Apart from grooming the coat and the facial hair, it is also crucial to include the eyes and ears in the cleaning and grooming routine of your Havanese. When it comes to the eyes, one problem that a lot of dogs encounter is tear staining. This problem is characterized by the staining that tends to grow in the area surrounding the canine's eyes.

Note that this condition is more prevalent in the Havanese breed. In some cases, it may look like mascara, which explodes beneath your puppy's eyes then caused the fur of his cheeks to develop stains. Fortunately, it is not that hard to deal with tear staining.

One way to cure it is to use a special whitening toothpaste. You may use it not only in tear staining but also in other areas surrounding the mouth that also have stains. Allow the toothpaste to stay in the area for one full night.

After that, you can wash it off the following day during the time when you are bathing him. It works in clearing up his unsightly stains. However, you have to make sure to avoid allowing the toothpaste to go directly to the eyes as it may cause the area to burn. You can also prevent that by using a cotton ball, which you have already dampened using a special eyewash. Use this damp cotton ball to wipe beneath the eyes.

If you want to prevent tear staining, then use an old toothbrush. Just dip it in water then use the toothbrush as a means of cleaning beneath his eyes every day. Ensure that you perform this step gently but with a touch of aggressiveness as it can increase your chance of maintaining the cleanliness of your dog's fur.

Apart from the tear staining, it is also a general rule for dog owners to clean the dirt from the corners of their puppy's or dogs' eyes. Perform such a step daily until you become more familiar with it without the risk of buildup. If, however, after exerting your DIY method of curing tear staining you still notice this problem, then maybe it is time to visit the vet.

Ears

The ears of your Havanese also need to be cleaned regularly. Note that just like other dogs who have long pendant ears that are also heavily feathered, there is a great chance for problems to arise if you do not clean the ears of your puppy regularly. To promote ease in cleaning the ears, apply an ear cleansing liquid in both ears prior to bathing him. Doing so is the key to loosening the wax in his ear, thereby promoting further ease once you begin cleaning them out using a cotton ball or Q-tip.

To clean up the ears of your Havanese, these simple steps and tips can help:

- Use one hand to hold one ear open.

- Use a moistened cotton ball or cloth to clean the insides of the ear flap using a cotton ball or moistened cloth.

- Pluck out any hair that grows within your dog's ear. You can do so with the help of your fingers. Just pluck out the hair using a pair of tweezers and your fingers. Also, remember to utilize a fresh cotton ball as well as a clean part of the washcloth you are using for every ear and eye.

- Do the ear cleaning process while your dog is on his side when he is still being groomed or dried. It can help a lot especially if you are worried that your Havanese will not stay still for such a task.

- Remove excess hair. If you notice that he has hair within both his ears, then it is highly likely that it will grow similar to how the remaining of your coat grows. However, constantly observe if the hair that grows within is already too excessive. In that case, you can use your fingers to pull out the coat. Fortunately, this will not hurt your dog.

Apart from the simple tips mentioned, it also helps if you visit your pet's vet. Your vet may be of help if you experience problems linked to the hair found within his ears.

Teeth

Another important aspect of Havanese grooming and care is cleaning up his teeth regularly. Note that similar to humans, the teeth of dogs are also prone to accumulating plaque that will eventually harden and turn into tartar. If you neglect the health and hygiene of your dog's teeth, then bacteria will grow, leading to infections.

With that in mind, make it a habit to brush the teeth of your dog regularly. Aside from the teeth, you also need to brush his gums and restore his fresh breath. It would already be a big help if you brush the teeth of your Havanese twice or thrice a week. If your pet is still young, then it helps to familiarize him with the habit of brushing. One way to do so is to scratch his muzzle and handle his mouth regularly. If you make a habit out of it, then soon enough, you can start rubbing both his gums and teeth using your finger.

The next thing that you can do once he gets used to that is to progress to gentle toothbrushing using a finger brush or tiny soft toothbrush. Avoid using a human toothpaste when brushing the teeth of your dog since it has detergent that may cause an upset stomach if he accidentally swallows it.

Invest in a canine toothpaste, instead. It refers to a special enzymatic toothpaste, which you can get at a pet supply store or from your vet. The good thing about it is that it is available in various flavors that your Havanese will surely find appealing, like liver, malt, and chicken. With that, he will start enjoying the process of brushing his teeth.

Nails

The nails of your Havanese will also need a regular trim. Note that if you left his nails unattended, then it is highly likely that they will grow too long. Remember, though, that your dog may not completely like the idea of you clipping or trimming his nails at first. It is the reason why you should start this routine while he is still young. The goal here is to familiarize him with the routine, so he can easily make it a part of his grooming routine. The nail trimming or clipping process should be done carefully. Do it one at a time. You also need to be extra cautious to avoid cutting the quick. If there are rough edges, then smooth them out using a nail file or emery board. You may also want to seek the help of your vet or a professional groomer if you feel like you can't do this task on your own. If you decide to handle this task, then remember that trimming his toenails is one of the most challenging parts. In this case, you may need to hold your Havanese down when you are clipping his toenails. It would be best to do the routine of clipping his toenails at the earliest possible age so he can get more familiar with this activity. To make this task a bit easier, you may want to invest in special clippers specifically meant for the toenails. These clippers look similar to a wire cutter. Again, look out for the quick when trimming or clipping the nails of your Havanese. You can easily identify the quick as it has different colors compared to the normal toenails. The specific part of your dog's toenail that you have to cut looks translucent and light. The quick, on the other hand, is darker, so you can easily determine which one you should avoid when clipping or trimming.

Conclusion

The Havanese is probably one of the most adorable small dog breeds that you can own. This dog looks adorable plus he has a lively and amazing personality that makes it a genuine joy to be with. The Havanese, therefore, has the strong potential of becoming a wonderful part of the family.

However, you have to make sure that you also provide him with the care and attention he needs for him to grow into the kind of dog you are hoping for him to be. As his new dog owner, you should be able to help raise him into the best version of the Havanese breed.

Fortunately, you have a better chance of doing so now that you have finished this book. All the information here, particularly when it comes to training him and improving his health, will definitely guide you all throughout your journey towards owning a Havanese and raising him into the most well-behaved and adorable dog you ever get the chance to know.

Look forward to wonderful days and years ahead with the playful, fun, adorable, and well-behaved Havanese as your companion with the help of this book.

Made in the USA
Monee, IL
24 September 2021